or exegete in history and the ways in which he defines his role by coming to productive terms with the pressures and immediacies of his own moment.

The other essays bring to specific problems of assessment and interpretation a finely adjusted sense of the critical uses of the historical category and the historical theses. Peter Elbow shows the function of Chaucerian irony as illustrated by two speeches in *Troilus and Criseyde*. Rudolf Gottfried examines the relationships of autobiography and art in Elizabethan literature; Francis Noel Lees applies historical interpretation to a poem by Dante Gabriel Rossetti; James E. Breslin shows how William Carlos Williams belongs in the Whitman tradition. These essays describe the range within which historical reconstruction serves not simply to provide useful information but to complete one's own immediate experience of a text.

Phillip Damon is Professor of English and Comparative Literature at the University of California at Berkeley.

Literary Criticism and Historical Understanding

LITERARY CRITICISM

AND

HISTORICAL UNDERSTANDING

❖ ❖ ❖

Selected Papers

from the English Institute

EDITED WITH A FOREWORD BY

PHILLIP DAMON

❖ ❖ ❖

1967

COLUMBIA UNIVERSITY PRESS

NEW YORK & LONDON

Acknowledgment is made to New Directions Publishing
Corporation for permission to quote material from William Carlos Williams's *The Collected Earlier Poems*
(copyright 1938, 1951 by William Carlos Williams) and
to Mr. M. B. Yeats, Macmillan and Co., Ltd., and The
Macmillan Company for permission to quote 4 lines from
William Butler Yeats's "The Choice" (copyright 1933
by The Macmillan Company, renewed 1961 by Bertha
Georgie Yeats).

Foreword

THE ESSAYS which comprise this volume were drawn from all
of the four conferences held at the twenty-fifth session of the
English Institute. The essays of Mr. Gottfried, Mr. Lees, and Mr.
Alexander come from the conference on Criticism and Biography, Mr. Elbow's from the conference on Chaucer's *Troilus and
Criseyde,* Mr. Breslin's from that on William Carlos Williams,
and my own from that on Criticism and History. To these have
been added Mr. Marsh's essay, which was written for inclusion in
this volume. As this account of origins will suggest, the title *Literary Criticism and Historical Understanding* asks for a broad
construction. The variousness with which its two terms are con-
joined from essay to essay is no doubt a mark of the topic's own
current complexities, one which even the author of a foreword
should try to resist smudging with programmatic generalities.
The past few years have brought forth maps, marching orders,
and assorted viatica for what Murray Krieger has called "the way
back to history and existence from the literary object contextually
considered"; but (as discussion at the twenty-fifth session bore
witness) orientation and sense of direction are still insistently individual matters. The volume comes out of this context, and its
essays embody some of the unity and a good deal of the diversity

to be found in this decade's much- (perhaps over-) advertised shifts in critical emphasis.

The first three essays take as their subject the historical and cultural variables which have operated on a variety of critical stances, past and present. The first essay proposes while the second and third merely expose, but all are concerned with the critic or exegete *in* history and the ways in which he defines his role by coming to productive terms with the pressures and immediacies of his own moment. The other essays bring to specific problems of assessment and interpretation a finely adjusted sense of the critical uses of the historical category and the historical thesis. They deal with limits as well as possibilities, and collectively describe the range within which historical reconstruction serves not simply to provide useful information but to complete one's own immediate experience of a text. The proper subject of all talk about literature is finally that point at which two experiences, the author's and the reader's, meet—the point which Northrop Frye describes in terms of "the tension or polarity between what a work of literature meant to its own time and what it means to us now." The preservation and utilization of this tension is what literary criticism and historical understanding are all about, and the essays all meet in an active concern with it.

Prevailing notions about the proper balance between these two meanings, the historical and the contemporary, have fluctuated during the past three or four decades; but they have been considerably stabler than the slogans and acerbities occasionally implied. One present burden for historians is achieving a firm hold on the fact that "contextualism" often embodied an essentially deeper feel for history than did the naturalist historicism which it aimed to supplant. Its insistence on the wholeness and autonomy of the work of literature was, in principle, an exploration of the way in which a work does in fact derive from and reflect the human condition. This was less a reaction against historical interpretation than an expanded reformulation of its potentialities and responsibilities. The "way back to history" (as Mr. Krieger himself has argued so well) requires new and more powerful interpretations of this reformulation, not polemical rejections of it. One can detect in these essays a persuasion that aesthetic wholeness and structural integrity are functions of larger systems of belief which define the concept of wholeness, and that these systems need to be understood historically as something that gets *into* a work of art. It is no paradox to hope that this kind of historical understanding will, in the end, lead us more directly back to the text itself than have some techniques of analysis more committed officially to concentration on intrinsic relations. The notion that the historian was a person who could assist the critic in his close reading by removing certain impediments to a work's "availability" (e.g., by telling him about the religious beliefs that made Antigone so set on burying Polyneices) may never have been very deeply held, but it did tend to spread itself on the record. The unsplittable historian *and* critic (I have H. D. F. Kitto in mind here) is the one who will show us that, as a matter of history, the relation between religious belief and art was as complicated for Sophocles as for T. S. Eliot, and that a real historical understanding of the play will not substitute a knowledge of Greek burial customs for a minute scrutiny of what Antigone says and does.

PHILLIP DAMON

University of California, Berkeley
February, 1967

Contents

❖ ❖ ❖

Historical Interpretation
and the History of Criticism
❖ ❖ ❖

ROBERT MARSH

It is becoming fashionable today to refer to that form of literary study concerned with understanding and explaining individual texts by the name of "hermeneutics." The fashion is stimu-
lated, one suspects, by the word's phonetic charm as well as by its
tendency to suggest the existence of a coherent, universal "science" of explaining verbal structures. I confess, however, that I
find the word somewhat awkward (perhaps because of its ety-
mological sense of "messages from the gods"), and for my purposes here I beg leave to use the commoner and humbler "interpretation," meaning by it something neither very unusual nor
very profound: simply the attempt to understand and explain
texts in a way that goes beyond the practical grammatical and
lexical exegesis of their verbal components. My aim is to confront
some issues specifically concerning the conceptual requirements
of what I shall call "historical interpretation." The adjective "historical" refers here not to the writing of *a history* of something or
to the establishment of broad epochal contexts for things, but
merely to the inquiry into particular facts and occurrences in
time as distinct from theorizing about universals. Thus historical
interpretation may be defined as the attempt to understand, in its
own terms, something written by a particular author at a particu-

lar time. The individual practitioner of this discipline may wish
also to judge that thing, before or after he understands it, or to
view it in all its possible states and relations as an embodiment of
eternal values or of recurrent anthropological patterns. Then
again he may not. He may decide that understanding it (and
being able to formulate that understanding) is difficult enough.
I do not contend that all interpretation must be historical in this
special sense; but it is, in my opinion, a discipline of considerable
intrinsic interest, as well as of practical importance for other dis-
ciplines, and its problems are challenging.

There is, indeed, a kind of radical historicist who says that we
are basically unable to understand things written in times other
than our own—except in our own terms. The metaphysical and
logical issues involved in that position are far too complicated to
attempt to resolve here, and I shall merely state what is to me a
commonplace truth: individual literary traits—traits absolutely
peculiar to individual works, writers, or societies or ages—must
always be, *as such,* impossible for anyone to understand, at any
time. I believe we should try to protect as much as possible of the
"sensible" individuality of the texts we examine, but to "understand" a text—at least in a way that can be formulated—is always
to render it *intelligible,* and this must be done in terms of generic
or specific characteristics shared by at least two individuals. The
crucial question, therefore, is whether human beings are capable
at all of accurately understanding things that may be different,
generically or specifically, from what they personally believe or
from their own private needs, responses, tastes, and so on. There
is perhaps no ultimate theoretical way to prove that capability;
but it is equally impossible to prove empirically that various

times or "ages" are unified and univocal wholes completely deter-
minant of the generic and specific characteristics men are and are
not capable of discussing, and only when that has been proved
should we be convinced of the futility of historical interpretation.
The discipline is difficult, but not impossible; like all inquiry (as
distinct from the application of systematic dogma) it yields
something less than absolute certitude, but it is not therefore useless or ignoble; its methods are rigorous (and often painful),
but they are not therefore unrewarding.

I shall not attempt to set forth a full account of what I take to
be the proper methods of historical inquiry in general. Different
aspects of the subject have been examined with penetration in recent years by Sir Karl Popper, William Dray, J. H. Hexter, and,
for literary interpretation specifically, by E. D. Hirsch, Jr., and
R. S. Crane.[1] For my purposes here only a few key principles
need to be stated. The first is that historical interpretation is a
task of discovery, not of speculation or deduction from theory. As

1. See Karl Popper, *The Poverty of Historicism* (London, 1957); Wil-
liam Dray, *Laws and Explanation in History* (Oxford, 1957); J. H. Hex-
ter, *Reappraisals in History* (London, 1961), especially Chapters 1 and 8;
E. D. Hirsch, Jr., *Validity in Interpretation* (forthcoming); R. S. Crane,
The Idea of the Humanities and Other Essays Critical and Historical (2
vols.; Chicago, 1967), especially the essays entitled "On Hypotheses in
'Historical Criticism': Apropos of Certain Contemporary Medievalists"
(II, 236–60) and "The Houyhnhnms, the Yahoos, and the History of
Ideas" (II, 261–82).

The argument of the present paper is an attempt to continue Professor
Crane's work on hypotheses in interpretation by carrying the discussion
into some general substantive questions about *kinds* of hypotheses and
how we come by them in the first place. I am indebted to him for helpful
suggestions, examples, and advice, but it should not be supposed that he
would necessarily endorse all that I have said.

such, it requires the examination and testing of different potential interpretations, because it is empirically demonstrable that no literary text is ever self-explanatory, and almost any explanation can be supposed to have some chance, however small, of being the right one as a matter of historical fact. Hence the second principle is that of the need for "multiple working hypotheses," [2] and its corollary is the proposition that, as historians, we have no way of determining ahead of time precisely how many potentially valid hypotheses there can be in a given case, even though we usually can, on the basis of ordinary common sense, denominate some as *unreasonable* (for example, that *King Lear* is a "descriptive poem" devoted to the visual phenomena of the medieval English countryside). Our problem, however, is to establish one interpretation as the most probable one, and this necessarily not only involves us in general questions of the nature of and rules for evaluating evidence but also brings us finally to the realization that we cannot be content with amassing positive support for a particular interpretation (important, of course, as that is) but must progressively eliminate all other reasonable possibilities. Hence the third principle is a negative one: no interpretation can be taken as likely to be the right one until all others with any serious claim to consideration have been carefully ruled out as historically unlikely on the basis of the evidence, internal and external.

We cannot continue very long, however, to speak of hypotheses

2. Crane (*Idea of the Humanities,* p. 236n.) cites T. C. Chamberlin, "The Method of Multiple Working Hypotheses," *Journal of Geology,* XXXIX (1931), 155–65, as providing him with especially important suggestions in the formulation of this principle of historical interpretation.

or possible interpretations only in general methodological terms. If one interpretation is more likely than all others it is so because of what it is substantively, because of its content. It seems obvious, in other words, that historical interpretation requires not only general standards of evidence and rules of procedure; it also requires concepts and ideas, in terms of which the interpreter formulates the special contents of his various possible interpretations. This is the requirement to which I should like to direct my attention. Taking my cue from Kant's statement (in a rather different context) that percepts without concepts are blind, just as surely as thought without empirical content is void, I begin with the premise that verbal structures and their parts cannot reveal any special intelligible characteristics—cannot yield "interpretations" at all—except in the light of the special concepts which the interpreter himself, with whatever degree of consciousness, brings to bear upon them. Stated in another way: as all inquiry and instruction must proceed in terms of what is already known or understood, no verbal structure is ever understood or explained except in terms of what one is already equipped, conceptually, to understand and explain. On this premise, then, the historical interpreter ought to be more than casually interested in the question of whether his "a priori" conceptual equipment is sufficient to what he supposes to be the basic facts of the literary situation in general. I wish to suggest that when he takes a view of the literary situation that inclines him toward explaining literary texts as human products—as "works" wrought in the medium of language that are determined in their essential characteristics *as* works by the productive efforts of particular men—the question of where he obtains, and how he justifies, his concepts is the most important question of all; and I shall argue further that, in confronting the very difficult problems implied in this question, he may find the study of the history of literary theory and criticism to have a special kind of value for him.

Now no one can be forced to view the literary situation in this way, in terms of human production or artistry,[3] if he declines to do so; but if we believe that particular human authors (rather than God or Nature or History or the Creative Logos or the universal responses of Humanity) are the determining, formative causes of the texts we look at, then we cannot reasonably limit ourselves to concepts that refer to them, say, simply as existing structures of linguistic and semantic elements. It is self-evident that we need specifically artistic concepts—concepts, that is, by which the texts, and parts and aspects of them, will become intelligible to us specifically as works of human art, as things determined in their "natures" as well as their existence by human artistic intentions and processes. Actually most of us do use artistic concepts in this sense in nearly every branch and mode of literary study. Even among systematic phenomenologists and existentialists one finds terms like "expression," "representation," and especially "content and form," which, in spite of their users' normally mechanistic and antiessentialistic doctrines, often retain some of

3. I am using the terms "art," "artistry," and "artistic" in as neutral a manner as possible, to signify only the very general principle that literary works—whatever else they may be—are "man made," without suggesting anything about the specific "natures" of such works. A "work of literary art" is thus simply anything a man can, or might try to, make with language. Perhaps only a certain limited number of different kinds of things can be made in language, but I know of no strictly empirical way to discover what that number might be.

the significance they have when used in their original or primary senses, namely, to indicate different kinds of human artistic tasks or processes. The trouble is that verbal structures are capable of seeming to be as works of art almost anything one wants them to be. This perhaps is a mark of our condition as fallen creatures, the fortunate result being that we have, and will continue to have, an enormous multiplicity and richness in our literary theory and criticism. One unfortunate result is the relative ease with which understanding and explaining the different kinds of artistic intentions and processes manifest in particular works may be confused with analyzing various "instances" of a single universal intention and process. The implications of this confusion for historical interpretation should be explored in some detail.

Considering the great diversity of commonly experienceable shapes, sizes, and qualities in the literature of any nation or any period (or even of any individual writer), we might expect historians to incline naturally toward the idea of a plurality of kinds of literary art. And yet a great deal of historical interpretation, as well as of criticism and literary aesthetics, has always been based, explicitly or implicitly, on the abstract notion that all verbal artistry—or at least all that given a special name like "poetry" or "imaginative literature"—is really the same sort of thing, whether the particular artists would ever admit it or not. Significantly, there has never been universal agreement about exactly what the one universal sort of thing is, but one widespread general concept, prevalent especially among those who concentrate on the "explication" of texts, is that all authors are engaged in saying something about a subject, in communicating or expressing (directly or indirectly) their perceptions, visions, feelings, attitudes, ideas, or arguments about something—in other words, in communicating or expressing "meaning." This is what they are supposed to be doing, that is, as verbal artists. I do not refer here to the obvious fact that literary works, like the events of life itself, usually will *have* "meaning"; I refer to a concept of *artistic intention.* Special versions of the concept have been especially popular in our time, but it has a long history, going as far back at least as the third book of the *Republic,* where even starkly mimetic drama is treated as a method—the worst of three methods—of quasi-philosophical discourse or exposition. Of course it is quite common in this familiar tradition to acknowledge at least two kinds of subject matter or meaning (scientific matter of fact and human understanding, or extension and intension, for example), and a number of natural, "historical," conventional, and personal ways of expressing them. Hence different special "varieties" of the one universal task are not necessarily ignored; it is not unusual in this tradition to work out lists of different "levels," "modes," "genres," "styles," and so on. The controlling problem nevertheless remains that of finding ways to understand and explain what an author has said or what meaning he has expressed or "spoken" in his text and perhaps also to give some account of how he has done it.

The irony is that the concept works. It will provide a means of rendering intelligible, as a work of art, virtually any literary text we might encounter. And, perhaps because it works so well, it has acquired the status of unquestionable axiom even among some interpreters and theorists of interpretation whom we might have expected to be more circumspect. Even, that is, for most of those scholars and critics who have sought to break away from some of the theoretical constrictions of the "new criticism" establishment (and do insist on the need, for example, to inquire into literal differences among authors' special intentions) the basic task of interpretation is still to explain what authors mean in their works. That is what, for them, "intention" itself means. It must be said that much interesting and useful exegesis and commentary has been produced in this general tradition; but it has always been of a sort that tends to beg the fundamental question of what, as a matter of historical fact, a particular author may have been up to as a verbal artist in constructing a particular work. An especially clear example is offered by E. D. Hirsch's recent discussion of "objective interpretation." [4] The argument turns on an interpretation of Wordsworth's "A Slumber Did My Spirit Seal," done with careful attention to the historical probabilities of Wordsworth's attitudes toward physical nature as the central means of ruling out alternative interpretations as probably wrong. My doubts about that interpretation, and about some aspects of the theory it illustrates, arise not from any quarrel with Hirsch's general standards of objectivity but from his presupposition of a quasi-philosophical intention when in fact that particular poem may have been intended as a dramatic rendering of a universal human situation in a sense in which there is no warrant whatsoever for identifying the speaker in any determinate way intellectually or emotionally with the author himself. That identification, in other words, involves a special notion about the *artistic nature* of the work. Should we not require the actual matter-of-fact elimination of the alternative possibilities before we embrace that notion? And what happens to Hirsch's central princi-

4. *PMLA*, LXXV (1960), 463-79.

ple of verification of meaning if it turns out that a given work is
probably not of a kind in which the author's own personal doctrines or attitudes need to be expressed at all? Hence even if we
wish, for some reason, to limit ourselves to questions of "verbal
meaning," to the special meanings an author intended particular
words and groups of words to have, the practical consequences
will sometimes be considerable if we are not too quick to assume
a philosophical or quasi-philosophical nature for all works of verbal art.[5]

I have singled out this general conceptual tradition for special
complaint, however, primarily to try to clarify the problem, not
to suggest that I think it alone is antithetical to genuine historical
interpretation. The same kind of question-begging obviously can
be attributed to anyone who uses one or another of several possible senses of, for example, "imitation" or "creation" to describe
what all literary artists are doing as artists. In other words, the
historical interpreter's problem is to *discover* what particular authors have done, artistically, in particular works; it is not to select
somehow a single theory or conception of literary art—from the
myriad that have been advanced (literature as symbolic social
action, or representation of everyday reality, or imitation of inner
human action, or imaginative re-creation of myth, or the tensional union of making with seeing and saying, or whatever)—
and then to apply it to all works to be interpreted, thus being able
to find alternative possibilities of interpretation only in possible

5. One kind of verification of this point—the distinction between language as action and language as saying—is clearly developed in Elder
Olson's essay "Hamlet and the Hermeneutics of Drama," *Modern Philol-
ogy,* LXI (1964), 225–37. See also J. L. Austin, "Performative Utter-
ances," in *Philosophical Papers* (Oxford, 1961), pp. 220–39.

variations within the normal range of the one universal art. My contention, therefore, is that any assumption, witting or unwitting, of the one true or comprehensive nature of literary art—or indeed of that of any special conventional category or "genre" (philosophical, rhetorical, poetic; lyric, drama, fiction; tragedy, comedy, romance; and so on)—not only is "unscholarly" in general but is inherently debilitating to the proper work of the historical interpreter. Clearly we must have and make use of concepts as well as percepts if we are going to say something intelligible about anything; in that sense, "theory" is universally necessary. But if literary works are indeed things whose essential "natures" and qualities are determined by the artistic efforts of particular men, the actual relevance or appropriateness of an artistic concept or a scheme of concepts to a particular text ought to be as much a matter of historical inquiry as anything else is; and for that inquiry we must find alternative possibilities in a plurality of fundamentally different kinds of literary art, not simply in the possible "varieties" of one kind.

This idea of fundamentally different kinds of literary art is essentially the idea of the different "formative" principles or causes involved in individual authors' construction of particular works. Hence it should be emphasized especially that from this point of view it is not enough simply to identify and reify what might be called the different historical conventions of literary art. I mean those various types and sizes, parts and devices, rules and regulations people have been naming, defining, and arranging in lists and hierarchies since the earliest beginnings of literary handbooks and encyclopedias. The total historical array of such things—ranging from codified devices and rules of sonantal combination and meter, through techniques of narration and dramatic presentation, to "receipts" for the construction of whole epics—is a vast, probably inexhaustible field for scholarly inquiry; and it is clearly important to know as much as we can about such things, just as it is important to know as much as we can about the historical conventions and principles of the language in which a work is written. This is knowledge, however, of conventional artistic *materials;* it can never, by itself, lead to understanding of the *formative* principles of particular works—of the special artistic intentions and processes of individual authors in particular cases. We still have the job of being aware, on the basis of something other than arbitrary dogma, of the different kinds of human artistry possible under any conventional head, the different special artistic uses any particular device, technique, or formula may be put to and the different ways it may be done.

Let me attempt to explain the problem a bit more concretely. It is not easy to "illustrate" adequately the principle of multiple artistic hypotheses in this radical sense if it is impossible to bring into view a large variety both of particular works and of fundamentally different artistic concepts to be applied to them, but perhaps I can indicate the sort of issue I have in mind with some typical examples.

A friend of mine informs me that he intends to write an essay on Jane Austen's *Sense and Sensibility* in which he hopes to show that this novel, as a work of art, is fundamentally different from Miss Austen's others. It is, he would argue, a special kind of "thesis" novel in which the characters and their actions have been selected and ordered so as to make clear to readers, in a "cautionary" way, the relative advantages and disadvantages in social life of certain states of mind, attitudes, and kinds of conduct. Practically speaking, all of her novels can be read, more or less successfully, in similar terms, and according to some literary theories this is the only intelligent way to read any novel; but my friend wishes to argue that of Miss Austen's six novels only *Sense and Sensibility,* as a matter of historical fact, *was constructed* (as a whole work) according to such artistic principles, the others having been constructed according to the principles of a special kind of "imitative" art—the portrayal of human situations supposed to have specific emotional powers in common human terms and the progressive narrative working out of the potentialities of such situations. What makes this sort of case significant, however, is that *Sense and Sensibility* too can be read, quite successfully, as an imitative narrative in this sense. To do so may, of course, necessitate considering it inferior, say, to *Pride and Prejudice;* but that is not the historical issue. If it is an inferior example of the kind, so be it; the question is, What kind *is* it—what *was* Jane Austen's artistic intention in constructing that work? And perhaps it was in fact to construct neither an imitative nor a "thesis" novel but a "history," representing, through fictional materials, actual social conditions of her time; or perhaps it was to present a philosophical exploration and resolution of the concrete dialectical interactions and conflicts of the ideas of "sense" and "sensibility." I am inclined to think that my friend's interpretation is very likely to be the right one historically, on the basis of what he has been able to find out about Miss Austen's own conceptions as well as on that of explaining all the "internal" characteristics of the work. But (as he would be the first to point out) these other kinds of verbal artistry are also completely reasonable possibilities for this work, and the historical interpreter must somehow be aware of such possibilities and be able to take them seriously, if he is to do his proper job.

I submit, moreover, that there are always possibilities of different kinds of artistic task and process *within* such general categories as I have just mentioned. This may be illustrated with two works that have frequently been compared by historians and critics, *Antony and Cleopatra* and *All for Love*. They are especially illuminating because of their common "story" and their common blank verse medium. It will be noted, first of all, that both plays may be conceived, literally, as "dramatic imitations of human action." Thus it would be relatively easy to examine both, for example, in terms of a somewhat organismic version of the Aristotelian schema of object, manner, and means of imitation and proper effect and explain their commonly observable differences of concrete features entirely as qualitative, technical, and circumstantial variations within the normal range of the single mimetic art. There are qualitative variations especially in the respective objects of imitation, in the actions, and in the dramatis personae and their characteristic statements and expressions of feeling. And these will account for most of the technical differences in the manners and means of imitation—for example, the closer adherence to the unities of time and place and the great degree of uniformity and regularity we observe in the diction and the meter of Dryden's play, no matter which character appears to be speaking in what situation, as contrasted with the "looseness" and diversity observable in the representational treatment and the language of Shakespeare's play. The technical representational and verbal differences *reflect*—"image" in a concrete physical way—the basic differences in the authors' special "conceptions" of their objects of imitation. Thus the fact that Dryden's blank verse is virtually always so constructed as to allow us to place the primary stresses on the "right" syllables (of polysyllabic words) without doing violence to the abstract iambic pattern of individual lines, whereas Shakespeare's very often is not, is a clear indication of the way in which the two playwrights have managed to actualize their different conceptions of their objects even down to the smallest elements of rhythm. Whatever differences may happen to remain unexplained or seem insufficiently explained in this mode of interpretation may then quite easily be referred to extrinsic circumstances—such as peculiarities of theater architecture and design, audience tastes, the conditions of the English language (and Dryden's well-known interest in regularizing and improving it as a language)—without calling into serious question the hypothesis about the specific kind of art at hand on which such circumstances are found to operate.

The method will work, undoubtedly; but there are reasons for thinking that these two plays may actually be fundamentally different kinds of things, both called tragedies properly enough because of their basically serious "subjects" and catastrophic "plots," but different, nevertheless, as examples of kinds of literary art. *Antony and Cleopatra* is perhaps indeed the product of a mimetic art of making structures of human action and character in the medium of language, a product, therefore, for which something like the distinctions of object, manner, and means of imitation would be the most appropriate ones. *All for Love,* on the other hand, might be more accurately viewed as the product of a kind of dramatic oratory, in which there is such uniformity

and regularity in the diction and meter, for example, because the
voice we hear is always actually that of the accomplished poet
himself addressing, "through the mouths of his characters," [6] an
audience of the "most judicious" on this old subject of great, un-
lawful love, and for which the most relevant concepts for historical interpretation are the "Ciceronian" rhetorical topics of the
poet's invention (or devised subject matter), his disposition of
it, and his style—topics Dryden himself applied even to the art of
painting. It presents, obviously, an imitation of human action;
but it is imitation in a special sense, one historically in no way
incompatible with the rhetorical topic of invention when that
topic is applied to "poetry." *All for Love,* in short, may be a thing
for which the quasi-Aristotelian poetic concepts are historically
off the mark as means of rendering it intelligible as a work of
human art. And *Antony and Cleopatra,* by the same token, is
probably a work for which the Ciceronian rhetorical topics are
not quite right.

The point, however, is not that I have here demonstrated the
true natures of these plays. Perhaps neither conceptual scheme
mentioned is historically appropriate to either play. Perhaps, for
example, a less organismic, less Platonized version of "mimetic"
art would be correct for both plays—or at least for Dryden's. Or
perhaps for Dryden's an Aristotelian conception of rhetorical art
(in which there is more emphasis on the poet's line of "argument" than on the established conventions of *dispositio* and *elo-
cutio*) would be better than the Ciceronian one. I think this is
not obviously the case, but the point is that the historical appro-

6. Cf. Wordsworth's Preface to *Lyrical Ballads* (N. C. Smith, ed.,
Wordsworth's Literary Criticism [London, 1905], p. 29).

priateness of any particular concept or scheme of concepts to any particular text is, or ought to be, a question of historical fact, not simply a question of dealing intelligibly with the work's common empirical details. There may be philosophical or practical reasons why an aesthetician or a critic (or pedagogue) will want to assume otherwise, but the historical interpreter's essential task is more demanding. It is, as I have said, to consider and eliminate, for a "given" work, all reasonable interpretative possibilities but the one historically most probable; and if this is indeed a valid principle of historical interpretation then one of his primary professional responsibilities is to be aware of the greatest possible number of really different and potentially relevant artistic concepts to work with. Surely it does no good to tell him that he must carefully and self-critically test and eliminate alternative interpretations unless he is able to think of a number of really different possibilities in the first place.

Of course, if we lived in a world where authors' artistic intentions and processes on particular occasions were always immediately obvious from the raw empirical details of their texts, and thus no text would ever lend itself to more than one reasonable artistic interpretation, our job would be considerably easier. But we are not in that world. And one of our most celebrated difficulties lies in the general likelihood that authors do not always clearly *know* what they are doing; and if they know they do not always tell us. In many cases the result is a frustrating reduction in the amount, and the immediate cogency, of available external evidence, the chief burden therefore falling very heavily on questions of relative adequacy to explain all the internal data and on comparison with other works for which external evidence is ampler. Such difficulties must not be minimized; but they are, after all, precisely what makes historical interpretation a matter of probability rather than absolute certainty, and they do not alter one basic fact: if he views literary texts as the products of human art, the historical interpreter needs as full a supply of "a priori" concepts of human artistic intentions and processes as he can command, and one that he can have some confidence will reflect the fundamental, literal differences of kinds of artistic tasks that men in various times and places actually have assumed and tried to perform (and may yet assume and try to perform) in the medium of language.

How, then, is he going to acquire that kind of confidence? It is plainly unreasonable to suppose that very many of us ought to rely on a belief in our "instinctive" understanding of things. The historical interpreter needs, I submit, some kind of deliberate training. But it is unlikely that he can expect to obtain what he needs from training in any one literary theory, conceptual tradition, or critical "system." For the problem is not simply to find, as an alternative to critical monism, a "diversitarian" theory or system, one that differentiates many kinds of artistic tasks, problems, forms, or "genres" but does so within a specific kind of theoretical framework—like that of Plato (whose plurality of artistic concepts I think has not been fully appreciated) or of Aristotle (who was perhaps the most literally differential of all) or of Kenneth Burke, or of anyone else. There is no reason to suppose that any particular system with many parts or distinctions must be more valuable than any one with few, unless there is some way to judge the historical adequacy and relevance of the particular parts of the particular system. To make that judgment we shall have to confront the question of the specific character of the parts (as they are determined by the broader framework of theoretical concepts and principles in which they appear) and assess their appropriateness, as a matter of historical fact, to the many texts we seek to interpret. And yet how could this be done independently of our awareness of the artistic natures of those very texts? To attempt direct assessment simply in terms of the common empirical characteristics of texts obviously will not do, since the problem is precisely one of deciding what such characteristics "mean" or how they function in artistic terms, and any single theory is capable, at least in the hands of a talented or industrious practitioner, of making some kind of artistic sense of any of the characteristics encountered. Even supposing, in other words, that a single theory or system might be adequate to the historical task, still I should not know how to find that out except by looking at the historical facts. But the primary historical facts for this problem are works of human art and the elements and circumstances of their being *as* works of art. Hence our very awareness of the primary facts (by which we might hope to assess the adequacy of our conceptual equipment empirically) depends on the variety of artistic concepts we are already able to bring to bear on texts.

Is there a remedy for this embarrassment? Should we simply conclude that the problem cannot be solved in any rationally deliberate way and cheerfully embrace one theory or kind of theory that happens to be fashionable or personally congenial and make the best of it? Probably our interpretations would not *always* be historically wrong, no matter what kinds of concepts we hap-

pened to use. I confess that sometimes this has seemed to me the
only possible way; and I have myself successively gone to school
to Plato, Coleridge, Aristotle, and a number of twentieth-century
critics in search of the most adequate theory to use for my historical purposes, in classroom and in print.

There is, however, a reasonable alternative worth taking seriously. And when I keep vividly in mind the special problems of
historical interpretation I cannot think of a better one. It is to become a student of the *history* of literary theory and criticism.
Certainly the study of the history of criticism can supply a very
large array of artistic concepts, of different conceptions and criteria of human literary intentions and processes, by which to
render texts intelligible as human products. But more than that
—only here are concepts of literary art readily available in a state
of potential independence of any particular theory or any one
kind of theory and thus essentially as instruments of interpretative discovery rather than deductive proof. Moreover, I should
argue that here there is far greater likelihood than can be expected from even the most diversitarian single system that one's
concepts will be sufficient to the total array of historical facts.
The controlling assumption in this argument is that the many
different things men *say* literary art is or ought to be are different
things it either actually is in fact or may become; and this includes the possibility that sometimes a particular work may be a
kind of thing accurately defined only in a time other than its
own. To reject this assumption is to claim to know beforehand
(either by a special theory of the true universal nature of literature or by a theory of absolute temporal determinism) which literary concepts can be valid and which cannot; and with that

claim we have returned to abstract dogma. I am suggesting, in short, that the most reliable deliberate means to the kind of conceptual confidence the historical interpreter needs for his special task is an inquiry into the many different things men have in fact said about the nature and value of literary art and its products.

To serve the purpose properly, however, this inquiry must be something quite different from what can be achieved by reading any of the available published histories of criticism. As historical interpreters of literary art we do not need *a history,* or what we might suppose to be *the* history, of literary criticism, conceived as having some kind of unified narrative form. We need a kind of inquiry that involves no special thesis or argument and that will indeed yield the fullest possible diversity of artistic principles and concepts in terms of which we may formulate our working hypotheses about the natures of particular works. Hence obviously it cannot be concerned with variations merely of terminology and of isolated statements of doctrine or opinion (on the assumption that all literary theorists and critics are really discussing the same thing, whether they like it or not). It must be an inquiry into differences of basic "philosophic" principles and of methods of reasoning, an inquiry based on the idea that by attempting to grasp a man's fundamental assumptions and his mode of thought, painfully difficult though this sometimes is, we are in a better position than we might be otherwise to determine the precise meanings of his terms and his various statements about his subject—to determine, for example, what "poetry" really means for him or just what kind of process he has in mind when he uses a term like "imitation," or "expression," or "creation," or a phrase like "tensional union of making with seeing and saying."

It must be an inquiry, moreover, into what men have said about all possible forms or sorts of literary objects and processes— philosophical, scientific, historical, poetic, rhetorical; theoretical, practical, productive; things of truth and goodness as well as of beauty; essays, treatises, dialogues, epistles; verse and prose; and so on indefinitely—not merely into what they have said about "poetry," or "imaginative" works, or "literature" in some restricted evaluative sense of that word. It will not matter, finally, whether many of the things said overtly deny the historical interpreter's own moral assumption that literary texts ought to be viewed as works of human art; for there is nothing to prevent an author from trying to construct something which obeys divine laws or natural laws, developing thus a work for which an originally antihumanistic or antiartistic theory provides the essential *artistic* task.

It should be emphasized that this is not an attempt to limit or control anyone's practical sources of *words* to use in talking about literature. Men's original sources of vocabulary, like their patterns of life and experience in general, must always be varied and unpredictable, even in the most uniformitarian societies. Although in the student's early training a systematic regimen of readings from the history of criticism would be valuable for acquiring specifically artistic terminology, the problem is to differentiate the artistic *concepts* that may be signified by critical terms, and it is ultimately as a way of acquiring a sense of *conceptual sufficiency*—something analogous to what Kant called "regulative ideas"—that the study of the history of criticism has its essential value in the professional historical study of literary art. We can never hope for absolute sufficiency, of course, precisely because our discipline is one of inquiry not of abstract theory, and we cannot be wholly certain that authors will never do things our conceptual equipment is not readily prepared to deal with in literal terms. But, if we pursue the study with seriousness and analytic care, I think we can hope, appropriately to the world of historical inquiry, for a sort of "probable sufficiency a priori," in which the degree of such probability is greater than can be obtained elsewhere—at least until that distant future time when the one true comprehensive system of literary concepts has been devised.

I do not wish to ignore the practical difficulties of what I am suggesting. Am I not asking a man to know a very great amount before he embarks on his specialized interpretative mission? Indeed; and the ideal historical interpreter surely will never exist as one man. Still we may always expect that the particular ignorance of one interpreter will frequently enough be balanced and corrected by the particular knowledge of another—in that continuing process of mutual inquiry that is the basis of what we call the community of scholarship. There are also some philosophic difficulties. Is the sort of inquiry into the history of criticism that I am advocating somehow possible without its own "a priori" concepts and ideas? Of course it is not, any more than it is possible without experience—of both nature and art. One thing, however, seems clear: whether they are specific "innate" features of the human mind, or must themselves be "derived" from intellectual experience, our concepts of different kinds of basic intellectual principles and methods must reflect the generic possibilities of human thought about art, much as our concepts of art per se reflect specific possibilities of human making; and they must, I think it is clear, be many rather than one.

What I have tried to say here will seem perfectly truistic to some readers, perversely heretical to others. To the latter not much can be said by way of apology. Many people have always found indefiniteness, lack of coherent theoretical system, and "pluralism" fearfully unintelligible. Some people I know even equate diversity with evil, unless it can be treated as dialectical opposition and hence resolved. "Historical interpretation" is for those who do not fear the prospect of finding real diversity in the world of literary art, or in any of its general conventional realms. In Chapter 17 of the *Poetics,* Aristotle—or someone, for the authenticity of that chapter has been disputed—remarks that convincing portrayal of different characters and their moral actions, feelings, and sentiments requires a man with either extraordinary talent for it or a touch of madness in him. Others have seen the need for divine inspiration, others the need for drugs. The historian of human art also may need such special help. But I should prefer to suppose that though we cannot all hope to make what some men can, or to see spontaneously what all the problems of making are, we can understand and explain the things men make when we have a way to discover the possibilities. And if this is not a simply foolish thing to suppose perhaps the historical interpretation of literary art can be aspired to even by those of us who can claim for ourselves only curiosity, periods of sobriety, and willingness to work.

History and Idea
in Renaissance Criticism
❖ ❖ ❖

PHILLIP DAMON

MY TOPIC lies uncomfortably close to the familiar conundrum about whether the Renaissance Mind was dominated by ideas of historical progress, by ideas of decay, by ideas of uniformitarianism, or by a special mixture of all three. I hope to seal my argument off from some of this problem's less productive complexities; and as a preliminary act of disengagement I shall associate myself with an impressively flat statement about the whole matter. It comes from a chapter entitled "The Historical Method" in Wimsatt and Brooks's *Literary Criticism: A Short History,* and is concerned with renaissance views of history in their relation to changing conceptions of literature.

The medieval and early Renaissance ages of criticism looked on literary norms as very safely fixed and on the history of literature— like that of civilization in general—as a decline from a Golden Age. The history of the world had exhibited a lamentable decline in "coherence." But the early seventeenth century in England saw the rapid rise, under Baconian auspices, of the idea that modern pygmy men might, by standing on the shoulders of ancient giants, reach even a little higher than they.[1]

1. W. K. Wimsatt and Cleanth Brooks, *Literary Criticism: A Short History* (New York, 1957), p. 523.

I think that these generalities cut through to some of the central facts that will concern the historian of literary criticism. Seventeenth-century England, influenced by intellectual pressures from sixteenth-century Italy, experienced a crucial and permanent revision of long-lived ideas about literary norms. This revision was closely associated with changing notions about the relation between past and present; that is, with a changing theory of history. And "Baconian auspices" seems a decent enough shorthand for the broad intellectual developments which included not only Bacon's empiricism but its less empirical antecedents and analogues in the speculations of Nicholas of Cusa and Giordano Bruno—speculations which involved some radically new ideas about both art and history. My own efforts to establish some connections between renaissance historical thinking and renaissance literary criticism are rather dogmatically grounded at these three points, and I was glad to find them so firmly encapsulated by such good authority.

However, I have a fourth point which I am going, ungratefully, to define by picking a minor quarrel with the picture of seventeenth-century Baconian pygmies standing on the shoulders of ancient giants. This particular motto or emblem was by way of being the official slogan of the twelfth-century brand of humanism associated with the School of Chartres; and Panofsky once used it as a symbol of the essential difference between the medieval and the renaissance sense of the past. He observed that the Chartrian dwarf was iconographically and conceptually similar to the apostles who sit on the prophets' shoulders in the cathedral at Chartres, and was, like them, the embodiment of a timeless, ahistorical view of the past which made the ancients seem almost like older and wiser contemporaries of the moderns.[2] Bacon never got around to saying, as Vives did, "They were not giants and we are not dwarfs," but he had his own ways of expressing the idea, one of them being the phrase which he presumably got from Bruno, "Truth is the daughter of Time." Fritz Saxl, looking for an emblem that reflected Bacon's understanding of that variously understood adage, found it in a design which shows Time dispersing the clouds to let the sun of Truth shine on a few great spirits like Socrates and most brilliantly of all on a modern.[3] Underneath is the relativistic motto, "In multitudine separavit eos et immutavit vias eorum." The dwarf-giant complex bespeaks (to quote Panofsky) "a sense of unbroken connection or even continuity with classical antiquity, linking the medieval German Empire to Julius Caesar, medieval music to Pythagoras, medieval philosophy to Plato and Aristotle, medieval grammar to Donatus." The renaissance emblem of Truth and Time (to quote Saxl) implies "the relative validity of intellectual perceptions (relative to their own time)." Between the two images lies the discovery of history in the modern sense or the emergence of "Baconian auspices," and their meanings are not interchangeable.

My excuse for belaboring an *obiter dictum* at this length is the precision with which it illustrates a very general problem in the study of renaissance thought. The problem has been more than adequately ventilated by historians of science, of economics, of social and political thought, and of painting, although less so by

2. "Renaissance and Renascences," *Kenyon Review*, VI (1944), 226.
3. "Veritas Filia Temporis," in *Philosophy and History: The Ernst Cassirer Festschrift* (New York, Harper Torchbooks, 1963), p. 218.

historians of literary criticism. It is the difficulty of relating forms
and formulas to the dynamics of renaissance culture, and the
consequent ease with which the historian can mistake a profoundly medieval idea for some new thing invented by the Renaissance. The critics of sixteenth-century Italy pose some quite
special hazards of this sort. They were in possession of ideas or
intuitions for which an adequate vocabulary and an adequate
generic format had not yet been developed, and their most powerful and original notions often present themselves in the shape
of an awkward formulaic struggle with old vocabularies and old
formats. Like the *docta ignorantia* of Nicholas of Cusa, with its
intimations of an experimental method whose processes it could
not label directly, cinquecento criticism is likely to be most revolutionary at those points where it looks most congestedly traditional. The limits and direction of critical discussion were heavily
conditioned by a fundamentally scholastic mode of textual commentary and by the surprisingly rigid conventions of the literary
quarrel. These formal pressures meant that personal emphases
and even personal excitement were often muted by the even flow
of routine serial comment on the *Poetics* and the *Epistle to the
Pisos*. The questions to which a given critic might bring an au-
thentically new insight tended to lose themselves in a thicket of
questions to which he brought no special illumination at all.
These pressures also meant that critical positions, whatever their
intrinsic subtlety, characteristically hardened at the surface into a
crust of easily dichotomized public "issues," and that noisy disjunctive slogans like Ancients or Moderns, Vergil or Homer,
Tasso or Ariosto, had a way of obscuring the quality and flavor
of the intellection that was going on behind them.

In short, it is frequently a difficult matter to describe or even to detect what is new or modern or renaissance in the critical theories of the Italian commentators and controversialists who are customarily described as the founders of modern criticism. There is in all of them a very great deal that is simply medieval aesthetic theory superficially adorned with Aristotelian terms and contemporary polemical flourishes; and some circumspection is required to avoid taking the verbal appearances for the conceptual reality and holding this sort of thing up as a renaissance novelty. Conversely, at least some of their work consists of new and strikingly prescient notions expressed in a language that evokes Aquinas, Bonaventure, and Hugh of St. Victor; and the historian who focuses too narrowly on the traditionality of the terms is likely to miss the originality of the thought. I suspect that difficulties of this sort explain why observations about their achievements are sometimes so offhandedly stipulational and appreciative, and why judgments about the originality or conventionality of particular critical statements are sometimes rather skewed. My impression is that assumptions about what constitutes the possible areas of continuity and discontinuity between medieval and renaissance poetics have not always been as rigorously tested as they might be.

A slightly timeworn but nevertheless serviceable distinction between medieval and renaissance modes of representing experience is based on the discovery of modern perspective both as a means of ordering the visual field in painting and as a means of coming to intellectual terms with the past in historiography. The distinction is too well known to require much discussion. The idea that the renaissance feel for distance, both spatial and temporal, be-

tween the observer and the thing observed represents a genuinely
new and controlling category of thought has been widely discussed and applied during the last couple of decades. In a recent
Italian edition of Panofsky's essays, there is a very long bibliography indeed on the subject. I shall have to take the general validity of the idea for granted, and limit myself to one summary
statement of it from Panofsky's introduction to his *Studies in
Iconology.*

No medieval man could see the civilization of antiquity as a phenomenon in itself, yet belonging to the past and historically detached
from the contemporary world—as a cultural cosmos to be investi-
gated and, if possible, reintegrated, instead of being a world of living
wonders or a mine of information. Just as it was impossible for the
Middle Ages to elaborate the modern system of perspective, which is
based on the realization of a fixed distance between the eye and the
object and thus enables the artist to build up comprehensive and
consistent images of things, just as impossible was it for them to
evolve the modern idea of history, which is based on the realization
of an intellectual distance between the present and the past, and thus
enables the scholar to build up comprehensive and consistent concepts of bygone periods.

In his *Four Stages of Renaissance Style,* Wylie Sypher discusses a
variety of renaissance literary and artistic phenomena in terms of
the "perspectived" approach to reality, and achieves generally
helpful results. When he comes to the great sixteenth-century
critics, however, something seems to go suddenly and almost
predictably wrong, and to do so in a way that typifies efforts to
present the commoner varieties of early Aristotelianism as analogous to the intellectualizing, rationalizing thrust of the *construzione legitima* in painting. To summarize his remarks with

injurious brevity, Professor Sypher finds his analogies in the way that Castelvetro's Aristotelian "unities" aimed "to reduce the structure of Renaissance 'regular drama' to an imitation of life seen from a designated point of view—the artificial perspective of a pseudo-Aristotelian canon confining the action to twelve hours, special motives, and noble characters." [4]

Now, the unities, during their lifetime as vital critical and dramaturgical realities, were used to support many different theories of art. The particular use in point here seems to me not only not analogous to the intellectual trends of renaissance perspectivism but part of an aesthetic theory that was quite antithetical to it. To force a slightly adventitious pun, Castelvetro's rules concerning time, place, and action have less in common with the illusionary distances of the *ars perspectiva* than with the real distances of the *ars prospectiva* implied in Alexander of Hales' egregiously medieval formula, "ars est prospiciens." [5] Art was "prospective" for Alexander, as for medieval aestheticians generally, because of the ontological gap between the pure, immaterial idea of the artist and its adulterated, material representation in the artifact. The *ars* consisted in the body of procedures which enabled the artist to look beyond his beloved idea and project it onto an intractable and rather hateful medium. "The artisan," says Bonaventure, "loves the statue which he has made, but hates a kind of knot of materiality which exists in it." [6] The notion of a "prospective" tension between the idea of the artist and the

4. Wylie Sypher, *Four Stages of Renaissance Style* (New York, 1955), pp. 74 ff.

5. *Summa*, I, 264 (Quaracchi ed.). See Edgar de Bruyne, *Etudes d'esthétique médiévale* (Bruges, 1946), III, 218.

6. *In Sap.*, III, v. 25. See de Bruyne, *Etudes,* III, 208.

medium which both objectified and spoiled it has some of its
roots in the aesthetic of Plotinus, for whom the type of the artist
was the sculptor, attempting with discouragingly approximate
success to impose his Neoplatonic idea on a lumpishly material
block of marble which did not figure at all in the genesis of the
idea and is seen by the sculptor primarily as an obstacle. Since
Plotinus seems in general to associate the artist's idea with es-
sences rather than images—with epistemological rather than
architectonic matters—his notions about its role as a principle of
order are rather vague, and there is a marked externality about
his conception of imaginative unity. The architect's task, he says,
is to stamp his indivisible inner idea upon the diverse "mass of
exterior matter," [7] as if his basic problem were the physical singularity of the bricks. Where an aesthetician less preoccupied with
an idealist metaphysic might see the problem in formal terms,
Plotinus is more inclined to see it as a direct wrestle with the
sheer fact of multiplicity.

Edgar de Bruyne has shown the tenacity with which this attitude maintained itself in the medieval *artes poeticae,* long after it
had been severed from some of its metaphysical moorings.[8]
When Geoffrey de Vinsauf says of the poet's idea, "status enim/
est prius archetypus quam sensilis," he would have us understand, among other things, that its pristine qualities have not yet
been smutched by the addition of *materia.* The poet's material
consists of items like *sententiae,* commonplaces, etymologies,
partly or wholly hypostatized faults and virtues—items which are
envisioned as hard, well-defined, discrete quanta of form and
meaning which the poet selects directly from reality rather as if

7. *Enneads,* I, 6, 3.   8. *Etudes,* III, 3 ff.

they were bricks. The Middle Ages had some fairly elaborate expressive theories of art, but when we descend from theory to specific cases and inquire what the poet's idea was supposed to do to
the separate entities amassed during the process of *inventio,* the
answers are decidedly modest, generally having to do with the
local rearrangement of parts. "In artificialibus," writes Bonaventure, "nihil impartitur agens passo, sed aufert vel mutat secun-
dum locum." [9] The poet does not transform, transvalue, or otherwise modify the things he selects from the world as objectively
given. With minor exceptions for extreme cases, they come to
him with their meanings, their truth, and their beauty solidly
embedded in them.

The general theoretical drift of Castelvetro's dramatic theory
belongs among the more obvious survivals of this medieval critical attitude. His pseudo-Aristotelian canons of time, place, and
action are, like the pseudo-Vergilian *rota* of the Middle Ages, the
vehicle for a conception of art opposed to the intellectual assumptions behind the *construzione legitima.* For Castelvetro, as for the
medieval writers on the art of poetry, poetic material is composed
of radically unmanipulable facts which are, so to speak, hoisted
bodily onto the stage for the contemplation of an audience which
is incapable of the slightest imaginative adjustments or suspen-
sions of disbelief. Castelvetro's ideal spectator is a preternaturally
dull mechanical who watches the action as if it were life, and is
unable to follow anything whose fidelity to ordinary experience is
not vouched for by his senses. Tell him that this lanthorn is the
moon or that two hours on the stage are supposed to represent an

9. *In Sentent.,* II, s.d. 7, p. 2, a. 2, q. 2. See de Bruyne, *Etudes,* III,
213.

entire day in the life of the characters, and he will be baffled and
angry. Why did Castelvetro interpret Aristotle's "revolution of
the sun" to mean twelve hours? Because, according to his calcu-
lations, this was as long as an audience could conceivably be expected to remain seated without needing to go to the bathroom.
Since stage time must correspond exactly to real time, it follows
that twelve hours is the maximum stretch of time that can be
represented by a dramatist who wishes to command belief. Why
must stage time equal real time? "Because it is not possible to
make the audience believe that several days and nights have
passed when they know through their senses that only a few
hours have passed, since no deception can take place in them
which the senses recognize as such." [10]

Ever since Spingarn, it has been customary to praise Castelvetro's interest in problems of stage representation as "modern";
and one can find histories in which he is presented as a kind of
theatrical type who was the first to bring a practical expertise to
bear on dramatic theory. Actually, he was an excellent specimen
of what Corneille insultingly called the "speculative critic." His
stage and his audience are a largely hypothetical construct—a
parable which is told in support of a highly traditional view of
art and which Castelvetro is quite ready to forget when it conflicts with theory. At the aesthetic level, his theory is functionally
similar to the theory which led Aquinas to class poetry as the
lowest form of knowledge and to speak of it as deficient in truth.
Aquinas was no despiser of poetry. It was simply that truth was
one, that it resided in substantial being rather than accidents, and
that (as Abelard put it) "the exterior sensuality of accidents

10. *Poetica d'Aristotele* (1576 ed.), p. 109.

prevents men from seeing the nature of things truly." There was nothing that the poet, with his images and his metaphors and his talk of "I" and "thou," could do about the low truth value of his material. He could not call upon a different order of belief and evaluation from the one his audience customarily applied in their transactions with the extrapoetic world. In *The Discarded Image,* C. S. Lewis spoke of the "ready-made meaning" which the universe was supposed to offer the medieval poet, and did an interesting job of illustrating how medieval aesthetics appealed to the absolute intelligence of God to deny that art had any autonomy with respect to this meaning. Castelvetro accomplished the same theoretical end by appealing to the absolute stupidity of his imaginary audience.

It has often been observed that renaissance theories of perspective began logically in a mathematical effort to provide objectively exact rules for representing space, and ended logically in an art conceived of as a triumph of the artist's subjective freedom, a demonstration not of his dependence on externally determined relations but of his ability to manipulate them in the interests of a private vision. In his essay "Perspective as Symbolic Form," Panofsky pointed out that sixteenth-century treatises on perspective deal with increasing frequency not just on the rules for the projection but on the implications involved in the choice of particular and even eccentric points of view. John White, in his discussion of Donatello's experiments with perspective, speaks of "messages for the intellect . . . which the emotional demands of the scene prevent him from giving more directly to the eye." [11]

11. "Developments in Renaissance Perspective, II," *Journal of the Warburg and Courtauld Institutes,* XIV (1951), 67.

This tight, tense relation between objective measurement and subjective freedom has been widely and I think persuasively seen as a characteristically renaissance phenomenon—the product of an aesthetic which relied on and exploited the fact that the viewer knew he was being deluded by the illusion of a third dimension on a flat surface. One thinks of the connection between *mens* and *mensura*—mentality and mensuration—which Cassirer found at the heart of the cosmological and historical theories of Cusanus and Ficino. Measurement, the establishment of exact relations in time and space, becomes in these philosophies both a form of the only true insight, which is self-explication, and the manifest sign of the autonomy of the human mind as the only value-creating agency in the universe. "The measuring mind," writes Cassirer in summarizing Cusanus' doctrine on this point, "can never do without fixed points and centers. But the choice of these points is not prescribed once and for all by the objective nature of things; rather it belongs to the freedom of the mind." [12] In the *Theologica Platonica,* Ficino insists that by measuring time, by seeing the course of history as progression and succession, man is mastering time and understanding the transcendent nature of his own soul. The ceaseless drive—the *continua discursio*—of the mind through singulars in a demonstration of its own nature recalls Cusanus' term *diagoge,* which like his coinage *possest* seems a calculated blow at medieval terminology. The medieval *anagoge* implied an upward movement of the intellect achieved by adopting an objectively established viewpoint which permitted the perception of sacramentally founded meaning in

12. *The Individual and the Cosmos in Renaissance Philosophy,* trans. Mario Domandi (New York, Harper Torchbooks, 1964), p. 177.

the world of natural objects. For Cusanus, the essential movement of the mind was not *ana* but *dia*—horizontal not vertical
—with the mind's own dynamic relating of particulars to each
other, its ability to see unity within diversity, being the mecha-
nism by which superior insight was achieved. And so, as Cassirer
observed, the question of perspective—a positive, critical awareness of cultural distances—begins to assume a theoretical importance in renaissance attitudes toward history. The individual's
ability to gauge the difference between modern and antique, between Christian and pagan, and to understand the difference in
relativistic terms as a prelude to integrating them into a unity
based on his own viewpoint, becomes a central issue in the philosophies of Cusanus and Ficino. As in painting, the feel for objective distance in history is closely allied with Neoplatonic per-
suasions about the autonomy of the human intellect as a genera-
tor of values.

The real nexus between sixteenth-century criticism and this
particular kind of intellectual control is not to be found in the
scholastic ontologism of Castelvetro's unities, but in the isolated
and half-smothered efforts to achieve a contemporarily meaningful and not just academically nominal definition of the poet's
hold on his materials in terms of the force and integrity of a subjective viewpoint. If one were going to make an *a priori* choice of
a sixteenth-century critic likely to have large ideas about perspective and point of view, he would probably choose Tasso. In his
book on Tasso, Ulrich Leo devoted a whole chapter, entitled
"Sehen und Gesehenes," to his preoccupation with the calculated
prehension of point of view and with the tense interpenetration
of subjective and objective within a visual field. When Italian art

historians want to talk about a poet who is vaguely like Tintoretto in his highly personal handling of distances, they often choose Tasso. In fact, Tasso comes closer than any of his contemporaries to offering us what might be called a mannerist literary criticism—a criticism that has felt some pressure from the violently wrenched perspectives and calculated visual distortions which accompany the intense inwardness of mannerist painting and its various analogues in the highly conceited styles of late sixteenth-century verse. I grant that very little of this appears in Tasso's prose by way of direct statement or connected argument. It constitutes a kind of submerged antitheory within his ostensibly quite conventional Platonized Aristotelianism. But if, as the saying goes, one should inspect theories for what they betray as well as for what they parade, this marginal aspect of Tasso's aesthetic perhaps deserves inspection. My major exhibits will be taken from his *Discourses on Poetic Art* and its later, fuller version, *Discourses on the Heroic Poem*.

The problem of choosing material for an epic seemed a particularly difficult one to Tasso, and at the beginning of the second book of the *Discourses on the Heroic Poem* he complains of "the shadows which darken the immense forest of poetic material" —the vast range of possible subjects and the mutability of attitudes toward them. "Therefore," he concludes, "if anyone is able to select, from among such a multitude of doubtful and uncertain things, that which is best and most fitted to receive ornament and beauty, he will be the wisest and most artful of men." The whole passage is an expansion of his more summary remarks in the earlier *Discourses* in support of the statement that the purpose of invention is "to select such matter as will be capable of receiving (*atta a ricevere*) that most excellent form which the artistry of the poet will seek to introduce into it." Professor Bernard Weinberg points out the traditional sound of the phrase "to select such matter," observes that Tasso says "select" rather than "invent" or "imagine," and concludes that he is thinking in terms of the traditional rhetoric in which "the poet does not make; he selects from nature a matter which has a nature of its own." [13] This point is well taken at the lexical level; Tasso's "scegliere materia" is unquestionably a literal rendering of the traditional Latin "eligere materiam." I think, however, that the question of what Tasso meant by "materia" is perhaps slightly more complicated than Professor Weinberg allows. In the *Discourses on the Heroic Poem,* the remark about material capable of receiving form occurs in the midst of an effort to distinguish between two separate meanings of the word "material." First, there is the material of the world of natural objects—the world which Tasso has just described as a field of choice for the epic poet. But there is in intellectual matters—"nelle cose intelletuale"—another kind of material which is analogous or proportionate to the first kind, a "non so che somigliante alla materia." It is, Tasso says, with respect to this second kind that we may define material as "a potency of our intellect that is capable of receiving (*atta a ricevere*) every form."

This "I don't know what" that resembles material strikes me as interesting. Ferruccio Ulivi, in his recent book on renaissance theories of imitation, treats it as an epistemological step in the progress from the shadowy forest of subject matter to the ordered

13. *A History of Literary Criticism in the Italian Renaissance* (Chicago, 1961), p. 649.

world of the poem. "To his eyes, 'material' appears turbid and multiform, and in order to present itself to the human consciousness, needs to transform itself into 'un non so che di somigliante,' and finally to rise to the level of artistic effect." [14] I doubt if the text will bear this interpretation. Tasso first describes material in its customary acceptation, then says there is another kind in intellectual matters, and abruptly drops the question by saying, "Let us leave these subtleties to the philosophers." No suggestion at all of a process in which one kind of material is changed into another kind. A second possibility would be that Tasso is alluding to his pet idea that contemplation is a form of action and therefore imitable under Aristotle's definition and consequently a fit subject for poetry. But he has already raised and firmly treated this notion in the first book of the *Discourses* and would not be likely to bring it up again in this rather mysterious way at the beginning of the second. And since the whole point of the business about contemplation depended on classing it among the actions of men, it would be working at cross-purposes here to call it a potency. The phrase "in intellectual matters" which introduces the reference to the "non so che" suggests a connection with Tasso's subsequent distinction between an intellectual fantasy and a sensory fantasy. He was led to offer this distinction in the course of denying, as against Mazzoni, that the true poet ever uses fantasy in the usual sense of conjuring up an unreal world of chimeras and flying horses. The true poet may use images which do not correspond to an observable reality, but this does not mean that he is writing fantasy. He is not addressing himself, like the dialectician or the scholastic theologian, to the composite

14. *L'imitazione nella poetica del Rinascimento* (Milan, 1959), p. 116.

part of the intellect which is concerned with proofs. He is work-ing like the mystic theologian, who proceeds not by proofs but by the intuitive and evocative use of images. Tasso compares the poetic image to the angelic portraits of the Pseudo-Dionysius and the four winged beasts of the Apocalypse: lion, calf, beast with "a face as a man," and eagle. Since images of this sort do refer to real things, albeit intelligible rather than sensory, they deserve to be classed as icastic rather than fantastic. However, if one insists on calling them fantastic, he ought at least to distinguish between a sensory fantasy and an intellectual fantasy—a distinction which Tasso claims is supported by Christian theologians and by the Neoplatonists though not by Plato or Aristotle. It is true, he con-cedes, that Aquinas denied that the poet used images in the same way as the mystic theologian, but he was thinking at the time of a kind of poetry which uses "weak proofs," and did not intend to include all kinds of poetry.

This distinction between a poetry of "weak proofs" and a poetry of the intellectual fantasy sounds like a very firm one, but they turn out to have at least one thing in common. As Tasso develops his ideas about them throughout the *Discourses,* they both appear to reflect his preoccupation with the metaphoric structure of the poetic conceit and the emblem. In the passage just cited, he talks about "weak proofs" in the traditional Aver-roistic sense of examples and similitudes, and sounds very much like a good Ramist rhetorician contrasting the "strict probation" of syllogistic logic with the "easy explication" of poetry's enthy-memes and *sententiae.* However, when he returns in the fifth book of the *Discourses* to the question of poetry as a special type of presentational logic, he refers to "silent proofs" rather than "weak proofs" and associates the probative force of poetry with a distinctly personal interpretation of the Longinian methods for achieving sublimity. He begins with what I take to be Longinus' category of amplification, and draws most of his examples from octaves of Petrarchan sonnets. It seems clear that he is interested in the intellectual pressure that builds up incrementally in the octave as the poem works toward the dramatic and conceptual resolutions of the *volta*. "In these verses," he concludes, "the cause of the *grandezza* is the way in which the meaning is left in suspense. It comes to the reader as to one who walks along a solitary way, and the inn seems farther away as long as the road is deserted and uninhabited. But many places to stop and refresh oneself make an even longer road seem short." As usual, the thinness of the context makes interpretation difficult, but Tasso seems to be saying that the "silent proof" of the octaves lies in their structure, their manner of collocating details, and that this structure "proves" or reinforces the conceit by acting as a sort of latent metaphor. The periodic sinuosities of the lines imitate the perspective of the traveler moving by obscure stages toward a goal.

The concept of intellectual fantasy develops in a roughly similar direction. Like many of Tasso's critical ideas, this one is at bottom a defense of *Gerusalemme Liberata*. What was biting him at this particular point was the imputation that, in mixing the historically verisimilar with marvelous improbabilities, he had created a monster and no true poem. What he is doing here is maintaining that his marvels are no less icastic than his history. (He had already shown that they were no less verisimilar by observing that the action of the poem took place under God's providence, and that nothing could be more like the truth than to attribute marvels to the power of God.) His choice of the Pseudo-Dionysian angels as an instance of intellectual fantasy is obviously tendentious, since they were the major source of Tasso's own much-maligned angels in the *Gerusalemme Liberata*. He does not indicate here how he would answer a critic who might concede him his angels but still object to Armida and Ismeno and inquire how these ostensibly wild inventions could be compared with the images of the mystic theologian and pressed into the service of spiritual hermeneutics. However, when he gets around to the question of poetic unity in the third book and reconsiders the marvelous not per se but as a function of aesthetic diversity, as a means of introducing a desirable sense of variety into a historical poem, he does sketch out the main lines of an argument. E. H. Gombrich has observed that the renaissance conception of higher meanings tended to differ from the exemplarism of medieval allegory in that the audience was invited not so much to rise to a new view of the object proposed as to rise above the object to a marginal participation in the creative act of the artist, whose capacity for unusual and unexpected juxtapositions—for unifying contraries—was among the most striking earthly analogues to the secret things of God.[15] Tasso compares the structure of his poem, specifically including its unhistorical infusion of celestial and infernal councils, prodigies, and incantations, with the structure of the world, "which includes in its bosom so many and diverse things and yet is one, one in its form and essence, one in the knot with which its parts are joined and bound together in discordant concord." This Neoplatonic pro-

15. "Icones Symbolicae: The Visual Image in Neo-Platonic Thought," *Journal of the Warburg and Courtauld Institutes,* XI (1948), 163.

gram for poetic unity is related to a view in which the analogical
function of experience did not (as it did for the Middle Ages)
lie primarily in its ability to provide singular, local, and specific
vestiges of God's purposes. It lay in its less differentiated status as
a matrix of greater and lesser unities which had been imposed on
diversity, a system of coincident opposites and reconciled contraries which were rationally conceivable models of the *discordia
concors* that was God. This was a view that had considerable cur-
rency in renaissance theories of the emblem, and it brings us back
to Tasso's second example of intellectual fantasy: the winged
beasts of the Evangelists.

In his dialogue *Conte* or *De l'Imprese,* Tasso, under his nom
de plume of Neapolitan Stranger, undertakes to show his inter-
locutor, Conte, that Scripture and theological tradition are full of
emblematic devices in which pictures of animals are used to ele-
vate the mind of the beholder to suprarational truths. During a
disquisition on lions, Conte remarks, "I observe that you have
passed by in silence the winged lion, presumably because it is
mystic and more appropriate to the theologian." "Yes," says the
Stranger, "that is precisely the reason, and so let us return to the
unwinged lion." Tasso is plainly thinking of the winged lion of
Mark in an emblematic context, and his deference to its mystic
undiscussability is based on the Neoplatonic notion that the jux-
taposition of incompatibles or union of contraries in emblematic
art was among the most potent tokens of arcane depth. Tasso's
use of the winged beasts to illustrate the compatibility of icasticity within a mystical context doubtless had affiliations with a variety of aesthetic and religious notions. But everything suggests
that in terms of a strictly personal relevance he would have

drawn very compelling support from Neoplatonic emblematics, which insisted that the material of the emblem must be strictly icastic but still made room for monsters like winged quadrupeds on the grounds that such images embodied the discordant harmonies which led the mind to higher things. In his emblem book, Ercole Tasso insists, as do all the major theorists, that the emblem must be most accurately "founded upon nature," except that it must accommodate what he calls "hyperbolical accretions" which, in the interest of deeper truths, do "some violence" to nature. As an instance of such accretions, he cites the addition of wings to unwinged animals. This seems to be Torquato's position in the *Conte.* He piously avoids analysis of "artificial" emblems but does not regard them as compromising his fundamental insistence on icasticity. I find it hard to think that this very contemporary tangent to the main lines of imitative theory was not somewhere in Tasso's mind when he formulated his ideas about an intellectual fantasy and illustrated it in the way he did.

In his *Pagan Mysteries in the Renaissance,* Edgar Wind showed how this emblematic emphasis on images of discordant concord can be related to the disequilibrium between iconography and psychology that characterizes so much later sixteenth-century painting. In discussing Michelangelo's *Leda,* he observes how a conceit, an old Neoplatonic pun, Leda as *leto,* the chosen vessel as Death, has penetrated a motif traditionally associated with the exuberant, life-bringing force of divine love, and expressed it in a "ruthless" image of gloom, lethargy, dully euphoric stupor. One is free to accept or not Wind's suggestion that the artist may have expected the initiated to see and understand the calculated resemblance between Leda and the figure of Night

on the Medici tomb. In either case, the tensions of the painting
remain as an instance of coincident opposites consciously embodied in style itself. The same processes are at work with an almost discursive clarity in Tasso's pastoral drama, *Aminta,* and I
am almost tempted to offer this dramatic idyll as a critical docu-
ment on the order of Theocritus' *Thalysia* or the *Eclogues* of
Dante and Giovanni del Virgilio. One recent expert says that the
Aminta "is the dream of an ideal world, entirely characterized by
courtly refinement, mysterious melodies, and soft and gentle tenderness." Another says, "Its outstanding characteristic is an often
crude realism." [16] I would say myself that its outstanding characteristic is a carefully contrived tension between these two opposed
qualities, and that the Neoplatonic artistic impulses which I have
attributed to Tasso as critic are involved in the tension. It cannot
be said that Tasso does not announce his purposes. In the first
interlude, the audience is greeted by Proteus and the theme of the
play is related to his shifting nature.

> Proteo son io, che transmutar sembianti
> E forme soglio variar sì spesso;
> E trovai l'arte onde notturna scena
> Cangia l'aspetto: e quinci Amore istesso
> Transforma in tante guise i vaghi amanti,
> Com' ogni carme, ed ogni storia è piena.

In the final interlude, the audience is dismissed by Pan amid allusions to inward, secret thoughts of love.

16. The citations are, respectively, from Vittorio Rossi, *Storia della
letteratura italiana* (Milan, 1924), p. 327, and Domenico Vittorini, *High
Points in the History of Italian Literature* (New York, 1958), p. 101.

> E se i pensieri in voi dormir non ponno,
> Sian gli affanni amorosi
> In vece a voi di placidi riposi;
> Né miri il vostro pianto aurora o luna.
> Il gran Pan vi licenzia: omai tacete,
> Alme serve d'Amor, fide e segrete.

"He who cannot attract Pan," wrote Pico in his *Conclusiones,* "approaches Proteus in vain." [17] This Neoplatonic adage means that one's introduction to Proteus, the ever-changing Many, assumes meaning only when directed toward a terminal sight of Pan, the Whole, the ultimate One. The adage is related to Pico's famous question, "Who would not admire this chameleon, man?" Man can change himself into whatever he wishes—plant, brute, angel—and through his metamorphoses, his involvement in change, reach the unchanging One in the depths of his own spirit.

When one understands that *Aminta* is a play which introduces us to a Neoplatonic Proteus in order to bring us at the end to a Neoplatonic Pan, some of its local puzzles become clear. At the end of the fourth act, when the theme of Aminta's "fortunate death" is at mid-career, the chorus summarizes the theme in an ode beginning,

> Ciò che Morte rallenta, Amor, ristringi,
> Tu nemico di pace, ella di guerra.

Editorial comment on the ode has stressed its obscurity, and Luigi Fasso's standard school edition flatly calls the opening lines

17. *Conclusiones DCCC: de modo intellegendi hymnos Orphei,* No. 28.

a *locus desperatus.* They have in fact sometimes been emended to make Love the enemy of war and Death the enemy of peace. But Tasso, like Michelangelo in the *Leda,* is plainly thinking of the Neoplatonic fusion of opposites comprehended in the figure of *Eros funéraire*—Amor as Lord of Death. In this emblematic complex, Amor is, like his mother, *Venus armata,* the patron of discord, and Death, like many another embodiment of Thanatos or Hypneros, is the procurer of peace. I shall not pursue Tasso's manipulation of this paradox, but simply assert that the ode functions very much like the motto on an *imprese,* and that the whole drama, in which "cose mortali" are metaphorically assimilated to the "giro eterno" through Aminta's "fortunata morte," is founded on the mystery of the One which is hidden within the Many.

And thus the mixture, noted above, of "gentle tenderness" and "crude realism"—the same disparity between iconography and psychology of which Wind speaks. The cold, meticulous formality of the drama's proportions and the chaste, unheightened lyricality of its verse seem almost too pure to be violated by action. A classicizing *convenienza* could hardly be carried further, but beneath the placid tenor of its rhetoric and its geometrically stylized gestures, Tasso's Arcadia is a troubled world. Of the famous choral ode, "O bella età de l'oro," we are told: "It is not solely an enthusiastic eulogy of the Arcadian past, but even more an invective against the poet's own period." [18] But it is not really a eulogy of Arcadia at all. The chorus is complaining of the con-

18. Erwin Panofsky, "Et in Arcadia Ego: On the Conception of Transcience in Poussin and Watteau," in *Philosophy and History,* p. 232.

science-ridden spirit of Arcadia, and contrasting it with a distant golden age before *Onor* had entered the world and the only law was "Do what you want." In the plot, we see cynicism, prurience, and a considerable capacity for violence ranged against a rather compulsive purity. In an exquisitely balanced, delicately modulated style, a disembodied cast of characters discusses rather than acts out a story of passionate extremities. As so often in mannerist art, one has the impression that the material's natural lineaments, emotional as well as structural, are being arbitrarily confined by the artist's private, highly intellectualistic attitudes. The formal tensions reflect Tasso's concern with the paradoxes of his Neoplatonic *desegno interno*—the conceit which put love inside death, peace inside violence, Pan inside Proteus, the stable One inside the turbulent Many.

And at the center of the action is Tirsi, a kind of tridentine Prospero, who operates inside the plot as controller of events and outside the plot as the voice of the poet reflecting on his own powers to control experience through art. Tirsi often puts a considerable strain on the "gentle tenderness" theory, as, for instance, when he tells Aminta that Silvia is to be found "ignuda e sola," suggests that if she remains obdurate his only solution is rape, and comes rather near to implying that this solution might have its own special pleasures. Tirsi is, despite his undoubted virtues, an obtrusive and rather morbid sensualist; and one can observe a characteristically mannerist wrenching of proportions when, on two occasions, he abruptly steps out of character and in monologues aimed directly at the audience reveals himself in considerable detail as Tasso, the poet who was to maintain that virtue does not reside in shades and forests but on the rocky heights, and who now lives in a Neoplatonic nirvana, his heart full of "questa semplice e devota Religion," meaning orthodox Christianity as defined by the Council of Trent. This is the poet as Proteus, both brute and angel, commenting with an extraordinary lucidity on his own notably schizophrenic involvement in the intellectual crisis of his time, and associating himself as poet with the human condition as his play represents it. This is the mannerist artist who can achieve a mystically complex meaning by "forcing nature" and subduing it to a style which mirrors his own precarious balance between the worlds of sense and spirit.

Aminta, with its individually lucid but obscurely related parts, is as hard to adjust to the more comfortable renaissance canons of imitation as the anatomy or the perspective of a Parmigianino painting. This is a style in which the artist's idea expressed itself in distortions, imbalances, incompletely resolved tensions within a context of meticulously rendered detail. Tasso's almost abstract comment on this style in *Aminta* seems as closely related to the emblematic paradoxes of Neoplatonic mysticism as anything in contemporaneous painting. The meaningful formal stresses of the play take us back to Tasso's theory of poetic unity as a *discordia concors* and to his technical interest in the emblematic conceit. This may suggest that it was no mere accident that he chose images evoking the coincidence of opposites as instances of his novel concept, the intellectual fantasy. And intellectual fantasy, if I am not mistaken, turns out to be closely related to the kind of poetic material which Tasso defined a potency of the intellect capable of receiving form. It may be, then, that his views on choosing material were not quite so traditional and scholastic as his terminology indicates. He seems to have been more in contact than any of his great contemporaries with an aesthetic which saw the poet's idea as something which could express itself through dislocations, odd viewpoints, improbable juxtapositions ostentatiously wished upon the visual data as the projection of a state of mind. This is a kind of artistic control, a kind of conceptual distance between eye and object, which is quite different from the kind of control envisaged by the unities in their purer Castelvetrian versions. For what such analogies are worth, I think that the tendencies which I have extracted from between the lines of Tasso's criticism are analogous to the psychologically based empiricism discoverable in the historical theories of sixteenth-century Neoplatonism, with their emphasis upon an ordering in time that was really an expression of the mind's effort to define itself. I am acutely aware of having turned Tasso into a mannerist critic more or less *malgré lui,* and I should not wish anyone to think that I think that I have described his theory of imitation. What I have done is assemble some scattered data which suggest to me that his ideas were not entirely circumscribed by his theory, and that he had moved beyond it in ways that can be related to some of the other intellectual developments which are usually somewhere in our minds when we use that confusing epithet, renaissance.

Roles of the Victorian Critic:
Matthew Arnold and John Ruskin

❖ ❖ ❖

EDWARD ALEXANDER

THE CAREER of Matthew Arnold holds a special fascination for
the modern literary mind because it was so definitely shaped by a
decision that literary orthodoxy has declared an error, even a be-
trayal. William Butler Yeats, that late Victorian attacker of most
things Victorian, gave pungent expression to at least two articles
of twentieth-century literary faith that seem relevant to Arnold's
life and work. In one of his famous pronouncements, Yeats said
that "we make out of the quarrel with others, rhetoric, but of the
quarrel with ourselves, poetry"; and in a poem called "The
Choice," he starkly defined the alternatives which faced the modern artist:

> The intellect of man is forced to choose
> Perfection of the life, or of the work,
> And if it take the second must refuse
> A heavenly mansion, raging in the dark.

I think that Arnold would have perfectly understood both of
Yeats's statements (though he would not have shared Yeats's
view that "curiosities about politics, about science, about history,
about religion" [1] were poetically impure and therefore mere rheto-

---

1. *The Autobiography of William Butler Yeats* (New York, 1958), p.
112.

ric). In the Preface to the 1853 edition of his poems, Arnold had
declared "the dialogue of the mind with itself" to be, however
unfortunately, the characteristic quality of modern literature—
which comprised, in Arnold's definition, everything since the decline of the great age of Greece. Arnold's "Empedocles on Etna,"
the title poem of his 1852 volume, was eminently a dialogue, or a
quarrel, of Arnold's mind with itself; and by reason of its inade-
quate subject, and its failure to issue in action and thereby rejoice
its readers, Arnold pronounced it a painful rather than a tragic
work and omitted it from the 1853 edition. The omission was the
first defeat of Arnold the poet by Arnold the critic, and for ob-
servant readers it foreshadowed the eventual triumph of the latter, for the strictures applied to "Empedocles on Etna" seemed
just as applicable to a great number of Arnold's poems, the best
of which express melancholy, vacillation, nostalgia, or at best a
resignation to peace where joy is wanting. William Wordsworth,
grandson of the poet, wrote to Henry Crabb Robinson that Arnold's preface "was curiously inconsistent with his practice: for I
suppose few writers are so intensely introspective as he is." [2]
Eventually, we know, Arnold did turn, at least to outward view,
from the quarrel with himself to the quarrel with others and became a consummate rhetorician.

I believe that Arnold would have understood Yeats's second
dictum as well as his first. The importance which he attached to
poetry hardly needs to be stressed: poetry was the most adequate
and satisfying expression of the human spirit, and also the most
truthful; it was the means of uniting and harmonizing in each

2. *Correspondence of Henry Crabb Robinson with the Wordsworth
Circle,* ed. Edith J. Morley (Oxford, 1927), II, 826.

man all the powers of human nature; it was again to become the complete director of life that it had been for the ancients.[3] "Perfection," whether of the life or the work, is a goal so often invoked by Arnold that it is almost the sign by which we know him. Not only his view of poetry, however, but the circumstances of his life put him in an excellent position to appreciate the terms of the choice between perfection of the life and of the work. In a letter of August, 1858, to his sister Jane, he writes, in justification of *Merope,* that tepid experiment with a great classical form, that he cannot attempt anything higher, cannot in fact do his best while his existence is hampered:

People do not understand what a temptation there is, if you cannot bear anything not *very good,* to transfer your operations to a region where form is everything. Perfection of a certain kind may there be attained, or at least approached, without knocking yourself to pieces, but to attain or approach perfection in the region of thought and feeling, and to unite this with perfection of form, demands not merely an effort and a labour, but an actual tearing of oneself to pieces, which one does not readily consent to . . . unless one can devote one's whole life to poetry.[4]

Arnold, then, disqualifies himself for the role of artist as hero because, though in a special sense, he chose perfection of the life over perfection of the work. As a rule, the first stanza of Yeats's poem is quoted in celebration of the nobility of the bitter sacrifice

3. *Letters to Arthur Hugh Clough,* ed. H. F. Lowry (London and New York, 1932), p. 124.

4. *Letters of Matthew Arnold, 1848–1888,* ed. G. W. E. Russell (New York, 1900), I, 72. Future references to this collection of letters will be given in the text in parentheses following each quotation. Yeats seems to have been much interested in this letter. See *Autobiography,* pp. 209, 210.

made by Yeats himself, or by Proust, or by Henry James, or by any of those who bravely refused to escape from art into life. To apply Yeats's verses to Arnold, however, is to find him guilty of retreating from art into life. Frank Kermode, who views the 1853 Preface as Arnold's apologia for the abandonment of poetry and the entrance into active life, says: "There is a sharp contrast here with Yeats, who, equally aware of the problem, and seeing it in very similar terms, knew why he wanted the management of men, understood his own guilt and felt conscious of damnation; he did not walk out of his dream, but simply extended it to include everything, and went on being a poet till he died." [5]

Even the most cursory comparison of Yeats's views on politics, science, history, and religion with those of Arnold will suggest the implications of Kermode's remark that Yeats extended his dream to include everything. Arnold both could not and would not indulge himself in this way. "I feel immensely," he wrote to Clough in 1853, "what I have (I believe) lost and choked by my treatment of myself and the studies to which I have addicted myself. But what ought I to have done in preference to what I have done? there is the question." [6] Disposed as he always is to touch social and political questions "only so far as they can be touched through poetry" (I, 271), he remembers what he told Clough in 1845 about the "one-sidedness" of aesthetics as social and political doctrine, [7] and resists the temptation to extend his dream to include everything, that is, to assert the unity between his feelings

5. *The Romantic Image* (London, 1961), p. 19. In *The Opposing Self* (New York, 1955), pp. xiii–xiv, Lionel Trilling comments on Yeats as the embodiment of the Scholar-Gipsy.

6. *Letters to Clough,* p. 136.   7. *Ibid,* p. 59.

and the facts of nature; the harmony between his imagination and ultimate truth; or the alliance between his instincts and the moral law. As a poet and a humanist, he resists the movement of science to oust literature from its primacy in education, but he remembers that unification of sensibility is desirable only if it means the wedding of emotion to truth and not dream:

Science has and will long have to be a divider and a separatist, breaking arbitrary and fanciful connections, and dissipating dreams of a premature and impossible unity. Still, science,—true science,—recognises in the bottom of her soul a law of ultimate fusion, of conciliation. To reach this, but to reach it legitimately, she tends. She draws, for instance, towards the same idea which fills her elder and diviner sister, poetry,—the idea of the substantial unity of man.[8]

When Yeats, as "A sixty year old smiling public man," enters the schoolroom ceremonially to inspect the operation of those prosaic modern educational methods he in fact so heartily despised he can think only of their antithesis in Maud Gonne; and of the incongruity of finding himself amongst the scarecrow philosophers and pedagogues. Arnold shared with Yeats Tolstoi's prejudice against "business documents and school-books" as material for poetry. In 1863 he wrote to his mother that "inspecting is a *little* too much as the business half of one's life in contradistinction to the inward and spiritual half of it, or I should be quite satisfied" (I, 223). In 1864 he told his publisher that he would like to write more, "but I am a scanty spring, and nearly choked just now by all the rubbish that Mr. Lowe's Revised Code (I am

8. *Lectures and Essays in Criticism,* ed. R. H. Super (Ann Arbor, 1962), p. 330.

a school-inspector) causes to be shot into me." [9] Yet when Arnold turned his experience of the classroom into literature, he stressed not the incongruity of the poet mired in a particularly disordered and grimy kind of life but the power of poetry to act, in the best and most literal sense, as a criticism of that life:

I once mentioned in a school-report, how a young man in one of our English training colleges having to paraphrase the passage in *Macbeth* beginning,
> "Can'st thou not minister to a mind diseased?"
turned this line into, "Can you not wait upon the lunatic?" And I remarked what a curious state of things it would be, if every pupil of our national schools knew, let us say, that the moon is two thousand one hundred and sixty miles in diameter, and thought at the same time that a good paraphrase for
> "Can'st thou not minister to a mind diseased?"
was, "Can you not wait upon the lunatic?" If one is driven to choose, I think I would rather have a young person ignorant about the moon's diameter, but aware that "Can you not wait upon the lunatic?" is bad, than a young person whose education had been such as to manage things the other way.[10]

If it is true that Arnold allowed the claims of life to override those of poetry, he never forgot, indeed he may almost be said to have taught us, that poetry is the most effective criticism of life.

II

What, then, was the nature of that life which Arnold chose in preference to art? We do not as yet have an adequate answer.

9. William E. Buckler, *Matthew Arnold's Books: Toward a Publishing Diary* (Geneva, 1958), p. 17.

10. *Discourses in America* (London, 1896), pp. 126–27.

Lionel Trilling, whose study of a quarter of a century ago remains the single most illuminating book on Arnold, has remarked that "there is really no biography of Arnold in the usual sense of the word";[11] and Frederic Faverty, in his 1956 survey of Arnold scholarship, noted that "of all the great Victorians Arnold has received the least adequate treatment in biography."[12] Some of the obstacles to a biography are external and circumstantial: the small amount of comment from Arnold himself on his first twenty-six years; the lack of information on the Marguerite episode; the world-wide dispersion of Arnold's correspondence and consequent absence of an edition of his letters; the lack of a complete bibliography.

But there are other and more intrinsic impediments. It was, according to his friend G. W. E. Russell, "Arnold's express wish that he might not be made the subject of a Biography" (I, vii). When a writer issues such a prohibition, he may do so because he has something embarrassing to hide—which in Arnold's case would be Marguerite—or because he has embarrassingly little to show. Richard Altick, in his recent book on English literary biography, implies that the second is Arnold's case when he mentions him among those writers who, because they are uninteresting as persons, "offer literary biographers challenges."[13]

But Arnold's unwillingness to be made the subject of a biography must be seen both as the outgrowth of his desire to hide his

11. Introduction to *The Portable Matthew Arnold* (New York, 1949), p. 34.

12. *The Victorian Poets: A Guide to Research,* ed. F. E. Faverty (Cambridge, Mass., 1956), p. 114.

13. Richard D. Altick, *Lives and Letters: A History of Literary Biography in England and America* (New York, 1965), p. 354.

life and as a means of winning his countrymen from their idolatries to the cause of light. In a letter of December, 1856, he tells his sister Jane that he has been escaping from the bustle of Eaton Place (his father-in-law's residence) to the secrecy of a friend's vacant apartment, and in doing so elevates his habit into a principle:

"Hide thy life," said Epicurus, and the exquisite zest there is in doing so can only be appreciated by those who, desiring to introduce some method into their lives, have suffered from the malicious pleasure the world takes in trying to distract them till they are as shatter-brained and empty-hearted as the world itself (I, 62–63).

This Epicurean notion of a hidden life which one conceals from others is related to, though not identical with, that Stoical conception of the "buried life" which must be preserved by concealment from one's own consciousness.

The notion of a hidden self seems to have been much in Arnold's mind in the early sixties. In 1862 and again in 1863 he copied into his notebooks Lacordaire's remark: "Se retirer en soi et en Dieu est la plus grande force qui soit au monde!" In the 1862 notebook we find also quoted Maurice de Guérin's praise of "une vie studieuse et cachée" as a continual celebration. In 1863 Arnold quotes Lacordaire on the way to achieve Christian detachment.[14] His final Oxford lecture of this year was on Joseph Joubert, "A French Coleridge." In giving, as was his custom, a thumbnail biography of his subject, Arnold noticed that Joubert

14. *The Note-Books of Matthew Arnold,* ed. H. F. Lowry, K. Young, W. H. Dunn (London and New York, 1952), pp. 16, 18, 17, 22. I am here indebted to Warren D. Anderson, *Matthew Arnold and the Classical Tradition* (Ann Arbor, 1965), p. 159.

cared more to perfect himself than to acquire a reputation, and stopped to explain the paucity of striking incident in his subject's life: " 'He has chosen,' Chateaubriand (adopting Epicurus' famous words) said of him, *'to hide his life.'* Of a life which its owner was bent on hiding there can be but little to tell." [15] It seems to me likely that, to some extent, Arnold put himself in Joubert's place, thought that he had kept his own life hidden, and that therefore a biographer could have but little to tell of it.

The decision to hide his life was for Arnold originally a method of self-preservation. In April of 1863, several months before delivering the Joubert lecture, he completed an article on Spinoza which asserted one of the two greatest doctrines of that thinker, who had lived even more obscurely than Joubert, to be his doctrine of self-preservation: "Man's very essence is the effort wherewith each man strives to maintain his own being. . . . Man's virtue is this very essence, so far as it is defined by this single effort to maintain his own being. . . . Happiness consists in a man's being able to maintain his own being." [16] Arnold clung to this decision to live obscurely, reminding himself of Epicurus' dictum throughout his life. The perfect life, he would write to his mother, is probably beyond the reach of most men, even of such men as Plato, yet surely Plato would have been less perfect had he been a man of action. When he was in America, Arnold wrote home to comment on the American obsession with movement and publicity that "I thank God it only confirms me in the desire to 'hide my life,' as the Greek philosopher recommended, as much as possible." Gladstone found Arnold the most inaccessible man he knew, and acquaintances complained that his elegies on

15. *Lectures and Essays in Criticism,* p. 185.   16. Quoted *ibid.,* p. 177.

persons who had been very close to him (like Clough and Stanley) were oddly lacking in "direct personal effusion" (I, 456; II, 267, 153, 229). When Arnold died, Jowett, who had known him as a gay, Olympian figure at Oxford and also as the mature writer and inspector of schools, the "Balliol man who had not got on," wrote in a letter: "No one ever united so much kindness and light-heartedness with so much strength. He was the most sensible man of genius whom I have ever known and the most free from personality." [17]

Not all of Arnold's readers have approved of his application of Epicurus' and Spinoza's strategy of self-preservation. Many, from Frederic Harrison to Mr. J. Hillis Miller, have taken it to be a confession of coldness and indifference toward his fellows, a strategy for escaping from life and experience. "Arnold's conscientiousness," writes Mr. Miller, "is that of the man who never takes the plunge into life because he fears all given ways of living are imposture, and will contaminate him." [18] But before we acquiesce in this view, should we not ask how it was that so little of life and of experience escaped from a man who was himself, we are asked to believe, so busy in escaping from them? The answer, I think, resides in the fact that the doctrine of the hidden life, which Arnold first adopted as a means of self-preservation, became also a means of dealing, as a critic, with the world about him; and for appreciating and even sympathizing with points of view and modes of life alien to his own as far as he could without actually adopting them.

17. *Life and Letters of Benjamin Jowett,* ed. E. Abbott and L. Campbell (London, 1897), I, 223.
18. *The Disappearance of God* (New York, 1965), p. 246.

III

In 1862 and 1863, as we have seen, Arnold was both thinking and writing about the "hidden life" as a means of protecting and ordering one's existence. His private correspondence shows that in October of 1863 something came to his attention which suggested that the spiritual discipline of detachment and self-effacement carried within itself the power of persuasion.

The October, 1863, number of the *Westminster Review* carried an article entitled "The Critical Character," which purported to review the critical works of John Ruskin and Matthew Arnold and to define the role of the ideal Victorian critic by comparing the relative effectiveness of the two men as critics. The reviewer, Samuel Reynolds, begins by subscribing to Renan's assertion that criticism has been an outgrowth of the nineteenth century. It exists by virtue of a new temper, characterized by freedom of thought, sympathy with both past and present, "foresight of the future," ability to distinguish the abiding from the transitory, and intellectual integrity. Having thus defined the critical character in the abstract, Reynolds chooses Arnold and Ruskin to illustrate his meaning, for Arnold, "in spite of some faults, . . . is the very best critic we possess" and Ruskin, "in spite of many great and noble qualities, . . . is one of the most deficient in the true critical temper."

Reynolds is far from hostile to Ruskin and anything but contemptuous of his intellectual power. On the contrary, he praises Ruskin for recalling the attention of his contemporaries to the civilization of the Middle Ages, which he refers to, in typical Victorian fashion, as if it were yesterday. Ruskin's entire distaste for the present is, to be sure, objectionable; but who—especially when he is under the spell of Ruskin's vivid contrast between a peaceful, contented past and a fevered, unsettled present—does not find it understandable and forgivable? Reynolds' deeper uneasiness is caused by the temper of mind revealed in Ruskin's writings. He is a reckless writer, whose ignorance of a subject never keeps him from formulating its theory and proclaiming the laws by which its study must absolutely be regulated. The disorderliness of his thought is perpetually at war with his stated intentions. "His sympathies and antipathies are often in ludicrous extremes; his whims and fancies are more than feminine in their number and absurdity." Whereas Arnold contents himself with judging the "adequacy" of the literature of each age, Ruskin must assume the role of the prophet and combine the function of the moralist and religious teacher with that of the critic. But his prophetic ardor moves Ruskin away from persuasion into a denunciation of sin which is so much the self-indulgence of the author that it can hardly be called criticism. Reynolds concludes that Ruskin's works are fatally flawed as criticism because they reflect too immediately and too well the personality of their author: "They have too deep an impress throughout of his self-will and eccentricity for us ever to accept his judgment without a degree of hesitation and mistrust. He is a thorough partisan; and appears to see no merit in what he dislikes, no faults in what he is pleased to admire."

Arnold, on the other hand, is the model of the critical temper. He is quite as bold and confident in his criticisms as Ruskin, "but he is confident without being self-willed, and bold without being paradoxical." Arnold always follows the rule of moderation and does justice to those whose wide differences from himself test his powers of sympathy. Having thus suggested the secret of Arnold's persuasiveness, the reviewer unwittingly attests to it by cheerfully accepting Arnold's classification of modern English literature in the third rank when two pages earlier he had chafed at Ruskin's undervaluing of modern English culture and civilization.[19]

It did not require this essay's use of Ruskin as a foil to himself to make Arnold aware of differences between them. They had not known each other at Oxford although Ruskin's last year at Christ Church coincided with Arnold's first in residence at Balliol. Arnold's first mention of Ruskin comes in a letter of March, 1856, to his sister Jane: "Have you seen Ruskin's new volume of *Modern Painters?* . . . Full of excellent *aperçus,* as usual, but the man and character too febrile, irritable, and weak to allow him to possess the *ordo concatenatioque veri*" (I, 58). In November of 1860, in the first of his Oxford lectures on translating Homer, Arnold took Ruskin to task for a remark in the discussion of the pathetic fallacy in *Modern Painters.* Ruskin had said, of the passage in the third book of the *Iliad* which follows Helen's speaking of her brothers, Castor and Pollux, who are in fact dead, as if they were yet alive, that "the poet has to speak of the earth in sadness, but he will not let that sadness affect or change his thoughts of it. No; though Castor and Pollux be dead, yet the earth is our mother still, fruitful, life-giving." Arnold mentions this piece of criticism as an instance where modern sentiment—in this case sentimentality—is foisted upon Homer, who did not share the "tender pantheism" of Mr. Ruskin. This subjective and

19. *Westminster Review,* LXXX (October, 1863), 468–82. I am indebted to Walter E. Houghton, editor of *The Wellesley Index to Victorian Periodicals,* for identifying the author of the article.

personal estimate of poetry reminds one, says Arnold, as does so
much of Ruskin's writing, of Sainte-Beuve's dictum: "Comme tout
genre de composition a son écueil particulier, *celui du genre ro-
manesque, c'est le faux.*" Arnold thus finds Ruskin guilty of
some of those sins he had in 1853 imputed to the Romantic poets:
obsession with the expression of isolated thoughts and images at
the expense of the construction of the whole, and the persistent
intrusion of personal peculiarities. Arnold had said that a poet is
"most fortunate, when he most entirely succeeds in effacing himself." [20] Ruskin was now raising for him the question of the role
of personality in criticism; perhaps the more strongly because
when Arnold met Ruskin for the first time, in June of 1863, he
quickly decided he "should never like him" (I, 228).

The *Westminster* essay was called to Arnold's attention by
Lady Rothschild. He was so pleased that he wrote to her to dis-
claim authorship: "It contains so much praise that you must have
thought I wrote it myself, except that I should hardly have called
myself by the hideous title of 'Professor'" (I, 231–32). On the
same day he described the essay in a letter to his mother as "the
strongest pronunciamento on my side there has yet been; almost
too strong for my liking, as it may provoke a feeling against me."
He would certainly keep the review on hand as a weapon against
his sister Jane, who had told him he was becoming "as dogmatic
as Ruskin. I told her the difference was that Ruskin was 'dogmatic and wrong,' and here is this charming reviewer who comes
to confirm me" (I, 233).

20. *On the Classical Tradition*, ed. R. H. Super (Ann Arbor, 1960),
pp. 102, 8. See also Arnold's letter of December, 1860: "Gradually I
mean to say boldly the truth about a great many English celebrities, and
begin with Ruskin in these lectures on Homer" (I, 147).

Arnold did not, of course, so badly misconstrue the review as to suppose it had complimented him for being dogmatic but right. Rather it confirmed and sharpened his conviction of the necessity to subordinate personality to the task of persuasion. Two weeks later, again writing to his mother, he says that "partly nature, partly time and study have . . . by this time taught me thoroughly the precious truth that everything turns upon one's exercising the power of *persuasion, of charm;* that without this all fury, energy, reasoning power, acquirement, are thrown away and only render their owner more miserable. Even in one's ridicule one must preserve a sweetness and good-humour" (I, 234).

In the first month of the new year Arnold wrote to his mother to express his satisfaction with the way in which his lecture on Joubert had called attention to its subject rather than to the brilliance of the essayist. With the praise accorded him by the *Westminster* obviously still in mind, Arnold reveals his new awareness that the strategy of hiding one's life, valuable as it is in itself, is also a most effective device of persuasion:

In the long-run one makes enemies by having one's brilliancy and ability praised; one can only get oneself really accepted by men by making oneself forgotten in the people and doctrines one recommends. I have had this much before my mind in doing the second part of my *French Eton.* I really want to *persuade* on this subject, and I have felt how necessary it was to keep down many and many sharp and telling things that rise to one's lips, and which one would gladly utter if one's object was to show one's own abilities (I, 255).

It should be noted that the people who needed to be persuaded by *A French Eton* were the very people attacked by Ruskin in *Unto This Last:* the opponents of state-action.

At the time he wrote this letter, Arnold had in mind and may have already begun to work on the Oxford lecture called "The Influence of Academies on National Spirit." Between the time of its delivery in June, 1864, and its publication in the *Cornhill,* Arnold deleted from the lecture, partly in deference to the principle stated above, partly, perhaps, in deference to his publisher, George Smith, "two or three pages . . . about the limits of criticism"—an odd expression to come from Arnold—and a portion of his criticism of Ruskin, a personal friend of Smith's.[21] The criticism of Ruskin which remained held him up as an illustration of that provinciality which pervades English criticism. Where Ruskin expresses his genius and his feelings, he is admirable; where he is forced back upon his intelligence and judgment, "the acquired, trained, communicable part in him," he becomes eccentric, immoderate, unbalanced.[22]

Within two months of the publication of the lecture on academies, Arnold lectured at Oxford on "The Functions of Criticism at the Present Time." In this remarkable piece, which obliterates the distinction between literary and social criticism and yet insists that the critic remain detached from practical affairs, Arnold justifies his desertion of poetry for criticism and distinguishes his role as a critic from that of his predecessors.

The beginning of the essay implies, though it does not state, a comparison between Arnold and those writers of the past whose careers prompt us to ask whether creative activity is in all circumstances preferable to critical activity. Granted that the inven-

21. Buckler, *Matthew Arnold's Books,* pp. 65–66, 170.
22. *Lectures and Essays in Criticism,* pp. 251–52.

tive faculty is in an absolute sense higher than the critical faculty, "Is it true that Johnson had better have gone on producing more *Irenes* instead of writing his *Lives of the Poets;*. . . is it certain that Wordsworth . . . was better employed in making his Ecclesiastical Sonnets than when he made his celebrated Preface?" Is it true, we are invited and tempted to add, that Arnold had better have gone on producing more *Meropes* instead of writing his *Essays in Criticism?* Only then we recall that the real question for Arnold was a much harder one: not whether to produce more *Meropes* but whether to produce more poems like "Empedocles on Etna." The dialogue of the mind with itself was not adequate poetry; criticism, the quarrel with others, would have to do its work before the poet could once more do something better than quarrel with himself.

Criticism, if it is to establish the order of ideas and of society in which poetry flourishes, must be disinterested in order to persuade others of its integrity. Other literary men had vitiated their criticism by failing to remain collected, by taking sides and being sucked into the "vortex" of practical affairs. Cobbett had "blackened" himself in this way, and he had been followed in his error by Carlyle with his *Latter-Day Pamphlets,* and by Ruskin with his "pugnacious political economy." [23]

The example of Ruskin was the most relevant to Arnold. Unlike Cobbett or Carlyle, Ruskin had begun his career as a man of letters, an art critic, and something of a poet (like Arnold he had won the Newdigate prize at Oxford). In 1860, having at last completed the final volume of *Modern Painters,* he turned to so-

23. *Ibid.,* pp. 259, 275.

cial criticism. He did so partly because of a puritanical conscience—no man, he said, could go on painting pictures in a
burning house—and partly because he had come to see, as Arnold
would, that the moral and physical education of a people is the
only foundation of great art, that "the art of any country *is the
exponent of its social and political virtues.*" He turned to his new
work with confidence in his own detachment: "I am untroubled
by any sort of care or anxiety, unconnected with any particular
interest or group of persons, unaffected by feelings of Party, of
Race, of social partialities, or of early prejudice. . . . Against the
charge, 'You live out of the world and cannot know *anything*
about it'—who do you suppose knows more about the Lake of
Geneva—I or the fish in it." Writing from self-imposed exile in
Chamouni, he composed a series of essays which began to be
published in the *Cornhill Magazine* late in 1860. They were a violent attack on the prevailing political economy—Ruskin called
them his "incendiary production"—and they aroused an indigna-
tion so violent that it forced Thackeray, the editor, to discontinue
the series. In 1862–63 Ruskin returned to the attack on political
economy in *Fraser's Magazine* only to be met by another storm
of criticism which forced J. A. Froude, the editor (and a good
friend of Arnold's), to discontinue the articles.

Ruskin, thrown into a state of severe depression, had discovered that physical detachment was no guarantee of spiritual detachment. Nor could he ever discover a middle ground between
Olympian detachment from the world's sufferings and total immersion of his soul in them. In March of 1863, when he had re-
treated from "English brutal avarice and stupidity" to the little
village of Mornex in High Savoy, he wrote:

The peace in which I am at present is only as if I had buried myself in a tuft of grass on a battlefield wet with blood, for the cry of the earth about me is in my ears continually if I did not lay my head to the very ground.

Little wonder, then, that he became "enraged and miserable," contemptuous and angry whenever he turned himself "upside down" to write of men and their social system: "I get so wild with contempt and anger when I think of these things that I can't write." One could live out of the world, Ruskin learned, and yet be only too much a part of it; and he could not find the means of involving himself in the affairs of the world without losing possession of his soul. In July, 1863, he wrote to Charles Norton that he was "tormented between the longing for lovely life and the sense of the terrific call of human crime for resistance and of human misery for help—though it seems to me as the voice of a river of blood which can but sweep me down in the midst of it, helpless." [24]

Arnold, writing to his sister three months later, and exactly a month after reading Reynolds' comparison of himself and Ruskin, says he is committed to working toward the transformation of the English spirit through literature, "freer perhaps in that sphere than I could be in any other, but with the risk always before me, if I cannot charm the wild beast of Philistinism, of being torn in pieces by him" (I, 240). Arnold did not want to suffer Ruskin's fate as a critic or as a man. He wanted to persuade and he wanted to hide and preserve his life from a world which could destroy it. In 1848, while reading the Bhagavad-Gita,

24. *The Works of John Ruskin,* ed. E. T. Cook and Alexander Wedderburn (London, 1909), XX, 39; XXXVI, 238–39, 344, 412; XVII, xl; XXXVI, 350, 348; XVII, xxxv; XXXVI, 450.

Arnold had told Clough that "the Indians distinguish between
. . . abandoning practice, and abandoning the fruits of action
and all respect thereto. This last is a supreme step." [25] By 1864,
when he came to write "The Function of Criticism at the Present
Time," Arnold had himself entered the realm of action and yet
kept his soul unspotted by it; had learned, in the words of "A
Summer Night," to "share in the world's toil" yet "keep free
from dust and soil"; and so he thought he saw in the Indian secret of self-preservation the secret of persuasion as well:

It will be said that it is a very subtle and indirect action which I am
. . . prescribing for criticism, and that, by embracing in this manner
the Indian virtue of detachment and abandoning the sphere of practical life, it condemns itself to a slow and obscure work. Slow and
obscure it may be, but it is the only proper work of criticism. [26]

Culture and Anarchy began to appear in the *Cornhill* in 1867,
and although it aroused murmurs, protests, and disagreements,
they amounted to nothing like the flood that had overwhelmed
Ruskin and the magazine's editor in 1860. Mr. Raymond Williams attributes the different reception to the fact that Arnold
"shirked extending his criticism of ideas to criticism of the social
and economic system from which they proceeded." [27] There
would, of course, be a piquant paradox in discovering that the
essential difference between Arnold and Ruskin lay in the fact
that Ruskin, whose only personal difficulty about money came
from an uneasy conscience about having too much of it, found
the root of all problems in economics, whereas Arnold, who was
so obsessed throughout life with money problems that he nagged

25. *Letters to Clough,* p. 71.
26. *Lectures and Essays in Criticism,* p. 274.
27. *Culture and Society: 1780–1950* (London, 1958), p. 146.

his publishers over every last penny of royalties, virtually ignored the economic aspect of his society's problems. But the crucial difference between them lay not in doctrine but in character, and in the partial reflection of character that was the critic's public personality. Arnold, having learned to live in the world and yet keep his inner life detached from it, advocated and practiced the subordination of self to society; Ruskin, living out of the world yet unable to detach his inner life from its workings, everywhere expresses and celebrates the autonomous personality in his work. Ruskin comes forth as the biblical prophet indifferent to public opinion or the need to charm; Arnold is made extraordinarily sensitive to the opinions of others by the conditions of his daily life, which oblige him to work in the midst of the very persons he is trying to convert.

The opinions of Arnold and Ruskin are similar on many points. They resemble each other in creating some image of the past as a criticism of the present; in making a healthy society the precondition of great art; in connecting art with the moral life; in equating government and cooperation with life, anarchy and competition with death. They also resemble each other in censuring many of the assumptions of laissez-faire economics. But where Ruskin, in *Unto This Last,* was telling manufacturers that they must institute equality of wages, must become as fathers to their employees, and be ready to render up their lives on behalf of these, Arnold, just two years later, in fighting against that monstrous offspring of the market mentality known as the educational system of "payment by results," was modestly suggesting that its perpetrator, Robert Lowe, was "a political economist of such force, that had he been by when the Lord of the harvest was besought 'to send labourers into his harvest,' he would certainly have remarked of that petition that it was 'a defiance of the laws of supply and demand,' and that the labourers should be left to come of themselves." [28]

The differences in the personalities of Arnold and Ruskin give rise to the most significant differences in their doctrines; and these can be readily understood by studying the implications of a paragraph in which Arnold for once asserts their agreement. In the penultimate paragraph of "Literature and Science" Arnold notes that the antique symmetry of the Greeks which Leonardo deplored the absence of in himself is wanting also to the Englishman, though he does not share Leonardo's regret over the fact. Arnold had been deploring since 1853 the English inability, in literature as in life, to subordinate the part to the whole, the irregularities of private experience to the symmetry of communal values. He now remarks how glaringly the fault appears in English architecture too:

Striking ideas we have, and well-executed details we have; but that high symmetry which, with satisfying and delightful effect, combines them, we seldom or never have. The glorious beauty of the Acropolis at Athens did not come from single fine things stuck about on that hill, a statue here, a gateway there;—no, it arose from all things being perfectly combined for a supreme total effect.

But Arnold's excursion into architectural criticism is curtailed by his omnipresent modesty: "Here we are coming to our friend Mr. Ruskin's province, and I will not intrude upon it, for he is its very sufficient guardian." [29]

28. *Democratic Education,* ed. R. H. Super (Ann Arbor, 1962), p. 243.

29. *Discourses in America,* pp. 132–34.

We must admit that Arnold is here being somewhat disingenuous. He is of course right to say that the inevitable correspondence between the character of a society and the character of its architecture is Ruskin's special province. But to imply that Ruskin would accept the opposition between the Greek and the English character, or that he would applaud Greek symmetry, or praise the ideal of perfection in art at all, is grossly to misrepresent him.

In *The Stones of Venice,* the final part of which was published in the same year (1853) as Arnold's Preface, Ruskin states it as a law of art that "no good work whatever can be perfect, and *the demand for perfection is always a sign of a misunderstanding of the ends of art.*" He takes imperfection, irregularity, deficiency, to be signs of both life and beauty; and charges those who would banish imperfection from art with trying "to destroy expression, to check exertion, to paralyze vitality." For Ruskin the Greek system of architectural ornament is a warning and not a model. The Greek system enslaved the workman because it denied him the expression of his personality in his art; it confined him to the composition of geometrical forms and symmetrical foliage, that is, to a kind of activity in which Ruskin can see no human faculty expressed. The medieval or Christian system, on the other hand, recognizing man's inherent weaknesses, also recognizes the value of the individual soul and encourages its expression in art. Ruskin's quarrel with his countrymen arises from the fact that they have chosen the pagan over the Christian system:

The modern English mind has this much in common with that of the Greek, that it intensely desires, in all things, the utmost completion or perfection compatible with their nature. This is a noble character in the abstract, but becomes ignoble when it causes us to forget the relative dignities of that nature itself, and to prefer the perfectness of the lower nature to the imperfection of the higher. . . . And therefore, while in all things that we see, or do, we are to desire perfection, . . . we are nevertheless not to set the meaner thing, in its narrow accomplishment, above the nobler thing, in its mighty progress; not to esteem smooth minuteness above shattered majesty; not to prefer mean victory to honourable defeat.[30]

Whatever name Ruskin gives to this creed of imperfection, it is surely recognizable as the Romanticism which Arnold attacked in his 1853 Preface and later, in its social form, as anarchy. Indeed, Ruskin's faith that out of the untutored, free, and individualistic efforts of many workmen toward self-expression arise great works of architecture may be likened to the faith of his antagonists, the laissez-faire economists, that an "invisible hand" guides the apparent anarchy of conflicting egoisms toward a harmonious and beneficial result.

From the Romantic point of view, as Ruskin expresses it, Arnold's life is a rejection of honorable defeat for mean victory, of Empedocles for Merope, of imperfect expression in the highest form for perfect expression in a lower; and the critical doctrine which was the outgrowth of this life seems an attempt to cut Shakespeare down to a Greek drama, and to fit Gothic cathedrals to the proportions of Greek temples. But perhaps, as Dwight Culler has recently shown,[31] there is limited usefulness in always judging Arnold from the point of view of Romanticism.

The criticism of Arnold's life that is implicit in Ruskin's doctrine of the imperfect is valid insofar as it shows his rejection of

30. *Works*, X, 202–4, 190–91.
31. *Imaginative Reason: The Poetry of Matthew Arnold* (New Haven, 1966), p. 20 and *passim*.

the Romantic conception of the self, but this rejection by no means proves that the pattern of Arnold's career was a narrowing of consciousness and awareness. Whereas "The Nature of Gothic" directs attention away from the work of art to the man who created it, the 1853 Preface asks the artist to turn his eyes from himself to the work of art that will rejoice his audience; it is thus an admission that the world of the individual consciousness is not the only world and that, in literature as in life, its claims must give way before those of the social world. The 1864 lecture on the functions of criticism, though it refuses to apply to the critic the criterion of action that the Preface had applied to the poet, is nevertheless a further assertion of the same truth. Arnold defines the crucial difference between his own critical role and Ruskin's when he makes the critic's effectiveness dependent upon his ability and willingness to subordinate his personality to the task of persuasion.

The degree to which Arnold did subordinate his personality to the requirements of persuasion may be seen in the little autobiography he includes in *Culture and Anarchy*. Unlike Ruskin or Mill or Newman, Arnold wrote no conventional autobiography describing his conversion (or "unconversion"). He had chosen, we remember, to hide his life; and yet, for a man with a hidden life, he made a great deal of what seems to be personality in his prose work after 1865. The same man who told his friends he did not wish to be made the subject of a biography could tell all England:

I myself am properly a Philistine,—Mr. Swinburne would add, the son of a Philistine. And although, through circumstances which will perhaps one day be known if ever the affecting history of my conversion comes to be written, I have, for the most part, broken with the ideas and the tea-meetings, of my own class, yet I have not, on that account, been brought much the nearer to the ideas and works of the Barbarians or of the Populace. Nevertheless, I never take a gun or a fishing-rod in my hands without feeling that I have in the ground of my nature the self-same seeds which, fostered by circumstances, do so much to make the Barbarian; and that, with the Barbarian's advantages, I might have rivalled him.

We recognize this as the description of a personality that has been shaped to the ends of persuasion; or, rather, it is the subordination of personality, in its changefulness and multiplicity, to character, to those stable elements in the individual's mind and soul which assign him to his moral category. Mr. John Holloway has demonstrated the degree to which Arnold's rhetoric depends upon the picture which he presents of his own personality. The description is no outright fabrication; we may simply refer to the many letters in which Arnold mentions his natural bent for fishing, to which, if he followed the line of least resistance, inertia would lead him. What Arnold has done is to reintroduce his personal experience in a different form from that which it takes in his subjective poetry. For he did not, like the servile workman in Ruskin's definition of classicism, surrender his freedom or his personality to a purely external authority; rather, he sought to substitute what he called his "best self" for his "ordinary self." "Our best self," Arnold says in *Culture and Anarchy,* "is not manifold, and vulgar, and unstable, and contentious, and ever-varying, but one, and noble, and secure, and peaceful, and the same for all mankind." [32]

32. *Culture and Anarchy,* ed. R. H. Super (Ann Arbor, 1965), pp. 144, 224. See Culler, *Imaginative Reason,* pp. 229–31.

We must remember that Arnold is the most elusive of writers. When we think to accuse him of wanting to establish authority in the form of a literary academy, he tells us that the wise believer in absolute values knows they are not to be embodied in brick and mortar institutions. When we are inclined to accuse him of falling into Carlyle's and Ruskin's error of placing exclusive stress on an inward transformation while calling all political forms mere machinery, we remember that he wrote to his mother in November, 1865: "I, who do not believe that the essential now to be done is to be done through this external machinery of Reform bills and extension of the franchise, yet look upon the outward movement as a necessary part of the far more vital inward one, and think it important accordingly."[33] When we read his severe attacks on Liberalism in the 1880s and abuse him for retreating into the conservatism of old age, we find him writing to his mother in December of 1885: "I hope that Lord J. Manners will get in for Leicestershire, and the Tory for Westmorland, though I should never myself vote for a Tory" (II, 354). Similarly, when we are inclined to label his patient and impartial temper merely the strategy of a man who wanted to persuade, we should remember that the man who was what Lionel Trilling calls a culture hero, "that is, a man who gives himself in full submission and sacrifice to his historical moment in order to comprehend and control the elements which that moment brings,"[34] was also one who believed that, to use his own words, "strength and success are possible to find by taking one's law, not from the

33. Letter of November 25, 1865, quoted by Super in *Culture and Anarchy*, pp. 413–14.
34. *The Portable Matthew Arnold*, p. 7.

form and pressure of the passing day, but from the living forces of our genuine nature." [35]

IV

The flexibility, detachment, and openness which constitute Arnold's disinterestedness and which set him apart from Ruskin are not things to be summoned at will; rather they grow out of a special experience of life. Why was it that whereas Ruskin could never free himself from the nagging conviction that "whenever I work selfishly . . . I am happy and well; but when I deny myself . . . and work at what seems useful, I get miserable and unwell," [36] Arnold could find his happiness in self-denial, and could write in 1862: "I sometimes grow impatient of getting old amidst a press of occupations and labour for which, after all, I was not born. Even my lectures are not work that I thoroughly like, and the work I do like is not very compatible with any other. But we are not here to have facilities found us for doing the work we like, but to make them"? (I, 193) I think that the answer lies in the nature of Arnold's experience, and that the part of Arnold's life which best explains his critical disinterestedness is that which is sometimes supposed to disprove its existence: namely, his experience as an inspector of schools and his practical efforts toward their reform.

The job of inspecting went against Arnold's natural bent and was adopted only so that he could marry. When he took the post in 1851, he thought he might get interested in the schools after a

35. *Essays, Letters, and Reviews,* ed. Fraser Neiman (Cambridge, Mass., 1960), p. 200.

36. *Works,* XXXV, 350.

time, but did not in any case expect to stay on the job for more than three or four years. Five years after he has been on the job, he says that he "half cannot half will not" throw himself into his work and therefore feels its weight doubly.[37] In January of 1859 he vows that he will not entirely give up his own work for any routine business. In the next month, on the eve of his visit to inspect the state system of elementary schools in France, he confesses to having "no special interest in the subject of public education" (I, 89, 90).

He returned from France committed to the cause of popular education. His experience there can perhaps be described by an account of Herder's French experience which Arnold copied into his notebook in 1864: "Herder awoke, in France—to the sentiment of human sympathy. The social spirit of France revealed to him the mission he can fulfill in the world. . . . Herder, without renouncing the superior ideas that were fermenting in his soul, conceived an ardent desire to imitate the *effective character* of French literature." [38] Arnold was now aware that literature, however grand its style, could not exercise a civilizing function on those who could not read English, much less Greek. The important bearing of Arnold's experience in France upon his ideas may be seen in the essay called "Democracy" which introduces his official report *The Popular Education of France*. Written in 1861, it contains all the ideas of *Culture and Anarchy,* minus the rhetorical development and the intrusive critical personality.

Arnold never fell in love with his work, and often tried, un-

37. *Unpublished Letters of Matthew Arnold,* ed. Arnold Whitridge (New Haven, 1923), p. 32.
38. *Note-Books,* pp. 26–27. (My translation.)

successfully, to change his post. But he was aware of, and thankful for, what he had seen and learned by virtue of his position. On November 21, 1869, the year of *Culture and Anarchy,* he told his mother that his long experience of visiting the nonconformist schools was the source of "all I have written on religious political and social subjects" (University of Virginia collection). It was so in several senses. It enabled him to see and know places and people he would not otherwise have seen and known; it gave him an immediate practical motive for advocating culture and deploring intellectual and social anarchy; it gave him a knowledge of practical affairs that made for the patience and detachment of his critical temper; and it firmly disciplined his ego by forcing him into plain and businesslike relations with indifferent persons through many hours of the week.

Arnold, as Trilling has pointed out, was one of the first writers to maintain a literary career, a respectable life in the world, and a large family, by nonliterary work. We have noticed, as did Arnold, the sacrifices and disadvantages which such an existence entailed; but it could also give unique strengths. Dr. Arnold once said of Coleridge:

I think, with all his faults, old Sam was more of a great man than anyone who has lived within the four seas in my memory. It is refreshing to see such a union of the highest philosophy and poetry, with so full a knowledge, on so many points at least, of particular facts. But yet there are marks enough that his mind was a little diseased by the want of a profession, and the consequent unsteadiness of his mind and purposes; it always seems to me that the very power of contemplation becomes impaired or perverted when it is made the main employment of life.[39]

39. Arthur P. Stanley, *Life of Thomas Arnold, D.D.* (London, 1904), p. 424.

Dr. Arnold's son, in 1861, inscribed in his notebook Bonstetten's saying that "nothing saves one in life but occupation and work." [40] Ruskin, in the same year, complained to a friend that he did not know what to do with himself: "If only a little round-headed cherub would tumble down through the clouds and tree-branches every morning . . . with an express order to do so and so tied under his wing, one would be more comfortable." [41] Neither nature nor circumstances would allow Arnold to await his cherub; he had to live and work in the world and to learn there the conditions in which man must shape his own fate and make his own good.

In conclusion, I would say that Arnold's character as a critic was shaped in part by the desire to subordinate his personality to the task of persuasion; but I would add that this character was more than a matter of rhetorical wiliness. It grew out of a particular experience of life which had taught Arnold that his own sacrifice of poetry was but a paradigm of the sacrifice that all men are called on to make: "I met daily in the schools with men and women discharging duties akin to mine, duties as irksome as mine, duties less well paid than mine, and I asked myself, Are they on roses? Would not they by nature prefer . . . to go where they liked and do what they liked, instead of being shut up in school?" For many of us, Arnold's laments over his work make of his life a paradigm of our own so near as to be chilling: "I am now at the work I dislike most in the world—looking over and marking examination papers" (I, 207). But the paradigm offers a consolation too. "To no people," Arnold once said, "does it so often happen to break in great measure with their vocation and

40. *Note-Books*, p. 12. See also *Letters*, I, 260.
41. *Works*, XVII, xxxix.

with the Muses, as to the men of letters. . . . But perhaps there is
no man . . . however positive and prosaic, who has not at some
time or other of his life, and in some form or other, felt something of that desire for the truth and beauty of things which
makes the Greek, the artist." [42]

42. *Essays, Letters, and Reviews,* pp. 308–9, 200.

Two Boethian Speeches
in *Troilus and Criseyde* and Chaucerian Irony
❖ ❖ ❖

PETER ELBOW

CHAUCER calls our attention to the problem of free will and determinism by Troilus' long speech in Book IV, and to the problem of whether man can have true happiness on earth by Criseyde's briefer one in Book III.[1] These abstract speeches may violate the conventions we call realistic and may be variously disparaged,[2] yet clearly they are deliberate: Chaucer departs in them from his principal source in Boccaccio's narrative to bring in philosophical material from Boethius.[3] We shall take the poet's cue and explore the meaning of the two speeches in relation to the poem. By exploring, in particular, the process by which we come to understand their full meaning, we can shed light on Chaucerian irony.

1. *Troilus and Criseyde,* IV, 958–1082, and III, 813–40, respectively. Reference and quotation follow the text in F. N. Robinson, *The Complete Works of Geoffrey Chaucer,* 2d ed. (London, 1957).

2. See, for example, H. S. Bennett, *Chaucer and the Fifteenth Century* (London, 1947), p. 61; and W. Curry, "Destiny in Troilus and Criseyde," in *Chaucer Criticism,* ed. R. J. Schoeck and J. Taylor (2 vols.; Notre Dame, 1961) II, 79.

3. R. K. Root, *The Book of Troilus and Criseyde* (Princeton, 1926), in his notes on the two speeches (see especially pp. 598–620) documents closely the sources in Boethius' *Consolation of Philosophy.* For an exact accounting, by lines, of the use of Boccaccio's *Il Filostrato,* see Robinson's headnote in his notes to Chaucer's poem, *Complete Works,* p. 389.

If we do not settle prematurely upon a final interpretation, we
find three stages in our process of understanding and responding
to these speeches. First we agree with them; then we are led to
disagree and see them ironically; yet in a third step we come to
see an irony in that very irony, and agree again more profoundly
with the speeches than we had at first. But we must nonetheless
finally take account of the strange fact that, when we are through
agreeing, disagreeing, and agreeing again, both positions somehow remain affirmed. Simple irony is saying one thing and
meaning another. What haunts in Chaucer is his ability to mean
both—to have it both ways. The final problem—that of Chaucerian irony—is that there is no joke.

I

The burden of Troilus' speech is that "al that comth, comth by
necessitee" (IV, 958). He is also concerned with two corollaries:
generally, that all men lack free will "every del" (1059); and
specifically, that it is his destiny to be forsaken by Criseyde
(959).

We begin by simply accepting his assertions of necessity as
serious argument and rhetoric. The same sentiments are repeated
in many different ways throughout the poem, not only by
Troilus and sometimes Pandarus, but most of all by the poet
himself. For example, when we read Troilus' speech in Book IV,
the striking opening of that book is probably still ringing in our
ears; the whole shape of the narrative is there ascribed to Fortune:

> But al to litel, weylaway the whyle,
> Lasteth swich joie, ythonked be Fortune,

> That semeth trewest whan she wol bygyle,
> And kan to fooles so hire song entune,
> That she hem hent and blent, traitour commune!
> And whan a wight is from hire whiel ythrowe,
> Than laugheth she, and maketh hym the mowe.

> From Troilus she gan hire brighte face
> Away to writhe, and tok of hym non heede,
> But caste hym clene out of his lady grace,
> And on hire whiel she sette up Diomede;
> For which right now my herte gynneth blede,
> And now my penne, allas! with which I write,
> Quaketh for drede of that I moste endite. (IV, 1–14)

Two stanzas near the beginning of the poem establish the range of rhetorical clothing for these sentiments:

> O blynde world, O blynde entencioun!
> How often falleth all the effect contraire
> Of surquidrie and foul presumpcioun;
> For caught is proud, and caught is debonaire.
> This Troilus is clomben on the staire,
> And litel weneth that he moot descenden;
> But alday faileth thing that fooles wenden.

> As proude Bayard gynneth for to skippe
> Out of the weye, so pryketh hym his corn,
> Til he a lasshe have of the longe whippe;
> Than thynketh he, "Though I praunce al byforn
> First in the trays, ful fat and newe shorn,
> Yet am I but an hors, and horses lawe
> I moot endure, and with my feres drawe" (I, 211–24)

Indeed, the poet seems quite seriously to hint that, because of the role of necessity, perhaps Criseyde is not as guilty as men have made her out to be.

In addition to the many direct ascriptions to Fortune by the poet, other aspects of the poem add to the sense of necessity. For example, through the serious use of courtly love, we are given a picture of Troilus, carefree and scornful of lovers, struck down helpless at his first sight of Criseyde. He resists in vain. And Criseyde, at her first sight of Troilus, exclaims "Who yaf me drynke?" (II, 651) We note also that Chaucer portrays the love story against the deeply fated story of Troy. Professor Curry notes these and many other direct and indirect references to fate, fortune, and destiny, and he concludes that "an absolutely inescapable necessity governs the progress of the story." [4]

But our agreement with Troilus' speech does not last. The psychological context leads us to see the speech in an ironic light. We begin to wonder whether the speech does not tell us more about Troilus than about free will and determinism. It not only helps tell us that he is despairing and looking for death, but it actually undermines our sense of determinism. For Troilus has already fully despaired and been put back on his feet by Pandarus with a plan for avoiding separation (IV, 220–658). Yet though there is no subsequent bad news, the speech shows him giving up again. Troilus feels Fortune as a powerful, active force pressing him to the ground, and himself powerless to resist. But we see only his own tendency to give up: Chaucer goes out of his way to show Troilus rather actively failing to exercise his possible freedom.

4. Curry, in *Chaucer Criticism,* p. 55. For the purposes of this paper, we can treat fate, fortune, and destiny simply as forms of necessity, and avoid the question of whether Chaucer distinguishes among them in the consistent way that Boethius does.

When we regard the substance of the speech logically rather than psychologically, we continue to be struck with its oddness. It slides quickly into a discussion of whether the necessity of events derives from God's foreknowledge or merely from the fact that they had to happen (cf. IV, 1008–15). But the premise of the second alternative, the question of why they had to happen, seems to be begged.

If we regard the speech historically, we see that these arguments for determinism, taken nearly verbatim from Boethius, are quoted without the Boethian context which goes on to prove free will: Chaucer gives Troilus arguments that Boethius set up for the purpose of knocking down.[5]

We find, in short, that the speech seems to make better dramatic than philosophic sense.[6] Troilus grasps the issue firmly in the first two lines, but then he gnaws and worries at it with fierce adolescent efforts to reason closely until the whole matter ends up seeming muddy. Troilus further undermines his speech by praying at the end for the gods please to make it all come out differently.

Aspects of narrative technique also make us see the irony in the speech. We soon notice that many events in the narrative are overdetermined. Events that the poet ascribes to Fortune are fully

5. See notes on the speech by Robinson, *Complete Works,* p. 830; and by Root, *Book of Troilus and Criseyde,* pp. 517–20. H. S. Bennett, *Chaucer and the Fifteenth Century,* p. 61, gives reasons for thinking that many in Chaucer's audience would have been familiar with Boethius' arguments.

6. H. R. Patch pursues this line of thinking at length and usually persuasively: *JEPG,* Vol. XVII; *MLR,* Vol. XXII; *Speculum,* Vol. VI.

explained otherwise. For example, the poet apostrophizes Fortune for the smoky rain that forced Criseyde to stay overnight at Pandarus' house:

> But O Fortune, executrice of wyrdes!
> O influences of thise hevenes hye!
> Soth is, that under God ye ben our hierdes,
> Though to us bestes ben the causes wrie.
> This mene I now, for she gan homward hye,
> But execute was all bisyde hire leve
> The goddes wil; for which she moste bleve.
>
> The bente moone with hire hornes pale,
> Saturne, and Jove, in Cancro joyned were,
> That swych a reyn from heven gan avale,
> That every maner woman that was there
> Had of that smoky reyn a verray feere;
> At which Pandare tho lough, and seyde thenne,
> "Now were it tyme a lady to gon henne!" (III, 617–30)

Chaucer need not bring Pandarus' chuckle so close on the heels of this apostrophe. And he need not have told us, just previously, that Pandarus waited for a moonless night, and one in which the clouds were piling up for a storm, before inviting Criseyde to dinner (III, 549 ff.). The poet calls further attention to human agency by Criseyde's protest, when invited, that perhaps she had better not come because of the rain (III, 562). Chaucer closes the account of the dinner invitation by raising a doubt that need not have occurred to us and, with a coy evasion, leaves it uppermost in our minds:

> Nought list my auctour fully to declare
> What that she thoughte whan he seyde so,

> That Troilus was out of towne yfare,
> As if he seyde therof soth or no;
> But that, withoute await, with hym to go,
> She graunted hym, sith he hire that bisoughte,
> And, as his nece, obeyed as hir oughte. (III, 575–81)

Chaucer pinpoints the moment when Criseyde first began to like Troilus more than anyone else, and again overdetermines it. The natural causes would suffice: before she sees Troilus ride by, Pandarus has been elaborately and subtly preparing the ground so that the sight of him makes her think fondly, we are told, of his prowess, social position, renown, intelligence, physique, nobleness, manhood, and most of all his pain and distress (II, 660 ff.). But Chaucer adds deterministic causes. First of all, the sight of him sinks from her eyes down into her heart and makes her exclaim, "Who yaf me drynke?" as though a force suddenly acts upon her. Secondly, Venus is in her seventh house at the time. And thirdly, as the poet says, the truth of the matter is that Venus was no enemy to Troilus at his birth (II, 650, 680 ff.).

Of course there is no purely logical or scientific reason why all these causes should not play a role together. Indeed, in our first stage of response, such passages give us no pause. But once our suspicions have been aroused, we become sensitive to the etiological congestion and the offhand tone. This narrative technique conditions us: when an event is attributed to Fortune but not described, we begin to read in the kind of natural circumstances that were earlier associated. We even get hints at how to read them in: for example (III, 1667–76), we are told that Fortune decided the time had come for a second blissful meeting. The circumstances, the poet says, were the same as before. Those circumstances were indeed memorable, but they involved not so much the agency of Fortune as the intricate and careful planning of Pandarus.

Characterization, as well as narrative technique, contributes to our ironic reading of the speech. Though Troilus is almost always passive, if not positively helpless, Chaucer consistently shows Criseyde working actively to maintain freedom and control. If she is led by Pandarus, she takes great care to be led only where she is prepared to go. After each of the many steps in the extended process of her yielding to Troilus, she stops and thinks about what she is doing in order to make sure she is still in control. We are given the reasons why she finally consents to see Troilus in Pandarus' house (III, 918–24), and it is quietly clear that, if this list did not include the secrecy of his coming and the safety of the place, she would not have proceeded. We see her exercise this veto on the occasion when Pandarus stages the passing of Troilus beneath her window. Pandarus sees that her pity is aroused; he "felte iren hoot and he bygan to smyte" (II, 1276). Wouldn't she now consent actually to speak to Troilus to ease his pain? But she says no, and there is nothing Pandarus can do. The affair remains at a standstill for a long while; indeed, it is the first time the narrative point of view moves back from its close chronological focus to let an indeterminate amount of time pass by (II, 1338–51).

If we look for the scene in which Criseyde's greatest inner turmoil is shown, we find that it is the long passage in Book II where she debates with herself whether for love she can give up her "maistrye" (II, 690–812). Her anxiety over the problem is portrayed not only by the length of the debate but also by the gradual acceleration of her changes of mind, till finally she can no longer think coherently, and goes off "to pleye." She is attracted to Troilus and to love, but " 'I am myn owene womman. . . . Shal noon housbande seyn to me "chek mat!". . . . Allas! syn I am free/ Shoulde I now love, and put in jupartie/ My sikernesse, and thrallen libertee?' " (II, 750 ff., 771 ff.)

We get our strongest sense of her freedom by seeing how she solves this problem. She gives in to love and Troilus because she finds him so obedient, discreet, and sensitive to both her feelings and her desires (III, 464–82). She loves because she is able to retain autonomy. Chaucer portrays her surrender more as an event that occurs self-consciously and wholly within her mind than as part of a process of interaction with Troilus. Indeed, Troilus seems rather left out. This impression is confirmed when we come to the first night of love. She undermines the strikingly aggressive tone he achieves on that occasion to assert, however sweetly, her autonomy:

> "Now be ye kaught, now is there but we twene!
> Now yeldeth you, for other bote is none!"
>
> .   .   .
>
> "Ne hadde I er now, my swete herte deere,
> Ben yold, ywis, I were now nought heere!" (III, 1206–11)

This control is later illustrated in their disagreement about whether she should leave Troy: she decides.

We now have many reasons for seeing Troilus' speech in an ironic light. But as the meanings in the speech and the poem develop and interact we begin to sense counterresponses, a new irony in the irony just seen, a deeper sense in which Troilus was right to say that all is necessary and men lack free will. This is the third stage in our response, and we can explore two sources: our final sense of Criseyde's character and our final sense of Chaucer's narrative technique.

In spite of Criseyde's autonomy, we eventually see her as a profound instance of unfree behavior. First we realize that her acquiescence to Diomede repeats the steps of her previous one to Troilus.[7] In both cases there is the slow capitulation involving many small steps over a long period of time. She characteristically asserts her control by refusing the favor asked while granting a smaller one of her choosing. When she tells Diomede that he may visit but not speak of love (V, 950), we can piece together the whole process, for it was by just such degrees that Troilus won her. She is perfectly sincere in such actions; she is not playing coy games. The matter lies deeper. Her wielding of agency and control serves actually to hide from herself the fact that she will always give in to a certain amount of importunity and shrewdness—the qualities of Troilus and Pandarus which Diomede so happily combines. This is not a random characteristic in her; Chaucer identifies it as "pite" (V, 824), one of the highest courtly virtues. It is the sufferings, in the end, of both Troilus and Diomede that eventually win her. Always she "means well" (e.g., V, 1004). Thus, her bemusement at the end is genuine: she does not know how it all happened and does not feel it is her doing.

This deeper absence of freedom in Criseyde is clearer if we

7. C. Muscatine, *Chaucer and the French Tradition* (Berkeley, 1957), p. 163.

look at it alongside the freedom we saw earlier. The two paradoxical ways of seeing her are illustrated by the two alternative
paths that would have saved her from her treachery. On the one
hand, her *freedom* led to her unfaithfulness: if she had sur-
rendered more of it to Troilus and followed his advice, they
would have lived happily ever after. But on the other hand, we
could blame her *lack of freedom:* while among the Greeks she
had to make a strong positive act to remain true, and we finally
see that this is precisely what she somehow lacks the freedom to
do. Though in control at any moment, she is powerless in the
long run. Is this only a manipulation of the empty truism that
people do what they do because of their character? If so, the
manipulation is Chaucer's, and he saves it from emptiness. For
by his portrayal of her character and by his shaping of the narrative, he creates a heavy sense of necessity in the way she responds
to Troilus and Diomede.

Chaucer's narrative technique adds to our final agreement with
Troilus' speech. Just as the details we learn of Diomede's winning of Criseyde were our first indications of her deeper lack of
freedom, so too the distancing narrative technique used in this
latter part of the poem also communicates a sense of the destined
shape of events. Instead of the method in the first three books
where the progress of the affair is atomized into its smallest steps,
and each is rendered in chronological order with full focus on the
present and none on the past or future, in Books IV and V
Chaucer forces upon us a detached view which gives a sense of
destiny. In the first three books, not even the narrator seems to
know what the future holds; here, we are constantly forced to
watch the slow coming about of what we already know and rue.

I am not just referring to the striking opening of Book IV where we are told that Fortune began to set up Diomede on her wheel. For we see the same process, and with greater effect, in the narrative structure of Book V. We start (V, 1–196) by watching Criseyde ride out of Troy with Diomede, we follow her, and we see at the end of her journey that, though she is sad and thinks only of Troilus, she nonetheless consents to give a familiarly civil response to Diomede's subtle urging. The end and the process leading to it are thereby suggested. Next (V, 197–686), staying in chronological time, we move back to Troy to watch Troilus for the first nine days of his wait. But toward the end of that period we get another suggestion of how things will work out: at Troilus' eager anticipation of her return, Pandarus mutters " 'Ye, haselwode! . . . God woot, refreyden may this hote fare,/ Er Calkas sende Troilus Criseyde!' " (V, 505–8) But then (V, 687–770), again not breaking time, we move back to Criseyde, and watch her thinking on the ninth day that she will return to Troilus no matter what the consequences. But in the middle of her thought that she will be true, in the middle of a scene, and in the middle of a stanza—and after three scene changes which have not broken the smooth flow of time—the narrator intrudes to jolt us ahead to the end of the whole story: she forgets Troy and Troilus:

> "But natheles, bityde what bityde,
> I shal to-morwe at nyght, by est or west,
> Out of this oost stele, on some manere syde,
> And gon with Troilus where as hym lest.
> This purpos wol ich holde, and this is best.

No fors of wikked tonges janglerie,
For evere on love han wrecches had envye.

"For whoso wol of every word take hede,
Or reulen hym by every wightes wit,
Ne shal he evere thryven, out of drede;
For that that some men blamen evere yit,
Lo, other manere folk commenden it.
And as for me, for al swich variaunce,
Felicite clepe I my suffisaunce.

"For which, withouten any wordes mo,
To Troie I wole, as for conclusioun."
But God it wot, er fully monthes two,
She was ful fer fro that entencioun!
For bothe Troilus and Troie town
Shal knotteles thorughout hire herte slide;
For she wol take a purpose for t'abyde. (V, 750–70)

This explicit revelation of the end functions as the ending not just of one story but of two, by the device of nesting one story within another. For we now turn back not to the Criseyde-Troilus story we had been following but to the interleaved Criseyde-Diomede story. It is only after watching that affair proceed to the end we already know (V, 771–1099) that we go back a second time to the ninth day, the point at which we modulated; and, having already viewed that sad interval of time from the point of view of Jove, we now must do so again, and watch Troilus' pathetic hope linger on through the long tenth day into the weeks that follow (V, 1100–end). The vantage point forced upon us by this narrative technique contributes to the final sense of necessity which has already been elicited by the handling of Criseyde's character—contributes, that is, to our final agreement with Troilus' speech that all is necessary.[8]

These three steps of responding may be slightly paradigmatic or ideal, but they are not fanciful. They are the three levels of complexity which actually inhere in the meanings of the words of the poem. For the second step, seeing the speech ironically, builds on the first one of responding to it literally; and the third step of more profound agreement is more profound precisely because it is built on the basis of our second, ironic response. Of course individual minds work quickly and idiosyncratically in the presence of a complex structure, and so my spelling out in detail of these three steps is likely to sound overintellectualized and neat. But though I do not therefore offer all this as an exact rendering of the details of every reader's reactions, I do maintain it is a paradigm of the kind of process that necessarily underlines a full response to the poem.

II

Criseyde's speech, which denies the possibility of true happiness on earth, elicits the same three stages of response; in fact, the two speeches come to function together at the end of the poem. We say yes to her speech first of all because, in itself, it is rather effective. It is shorter, firmer, and clearer than Troilus'. It closes with

8. Determinism does not by necessary logic inhere in this God's-eye foresight. Though Troilus suspects it does, Chaucer, in fact, omitted precisely those passages in Boethius where Dame Philosophy shows that God's foreknowledge does not cause necessity. The complex relation between detachment and determinism is explored by M. W. Bloomfield, in *Chaucer Criticism*, pp. 204 ff.; see also C. A. Owen, Jr., *ibid.*, pp. 165–66.

the same logical device Troilus uses: asserting that all possibilities can be gathered into an "either/or" set, and then showing that the conclusion follows from both:

> Either he woot that thow, joie, art muable
> Or woot it nought; it mot been oon of tweye.
> Now if he woot it nought, how may he seye
> That he hath verray joie and selynesse,
> That is of ignoraunce ay in derknesse?

> Now if he woot that joie is transitorie,
> As every joie of worldly thyng mot flee,
> Than every tyme he that hath in memorie,
> The drede of lesing maketh hym that he
> May in no perfit selynesse be.

We assent to the neat alternatives because they fit Troilus so well. He is strikingly ignorant of the transitory nature of his happy condition, both in the beginning when he scorns love, and at the height of his success with Criseyde. And when he is hoping and expecting her to return from the Greeks, his ignorance is even more affecting. Yet when he learned that she must leave—learned that their joy must be transitory—the knowledge destroyed for him any possibility of happiness in their remaining time.

Thus like Troilus' speech, hers is first accepted on its own terms as serious rhetoric carrying simple, abstract truth value for the poem. But we begin to sense an ironic reading, as we did in Troilus' speech, when we begin to sense its paradoxical relation to the dramatic context. These somber sentiments issue on the occasion of Pandarus' most gratuitously trumped-up story of jealousy, in his elaborate staging that brings the lovers happily to bed. A graver joy adds to these ironic circumstances to undermine her pessimistic speech. For it stands near the center of Book III which Chaucer distinguished from the others by an elegant symmetry born of the arrangement of passages expressing lofty joy.[9] The opening and closing of the Book are matched with deeply serious hymns telling how love creates perfect joy and holds all things in harmony. Ironically, her speech serves to introduce the portrayal of the consummation of their love which forms the central portion of the poem as well as the Book. In rendering this extended scene, Chaucer emphasizes the perfection of their joy. This impression is heightened rather than undermined by the momentary bewilderment of the lovers: "'O swete,/ Clippe ich you thus, or elles I it meete?'" (III, 1344) The quiet insistence on physicality—picked up even in the word "clippe" above—gives the opposite of a dreamlike or unreal quality. Finally, the poet himself consciously addresses the question of perfect joy:

> Nought nedeth it to you, syn they ben met,
> To axe at me if that they blithe were;
> For if it erst was wel, tho was it bet
> A thousand fold; this nedeth nought enquere.
> Agon was every sorwe and every feere;
> And bothe ywis, they hadde, and so they wende,
> As muche joie as herte may comprehende.
>
> This is no litel thing of for to seye;
> This passeth every wit for to devyse;
> For ech of hem gan otheres lust obeye.
> Felicite, which that these clerkes wise
> Comenden so, ne may nought here suffise;

9. Owen, in *Chaucer Criticism*, explores these symmetries.

> This joie may nought writen be with inke;
> This passeth all that herte may bythynke. (III, 1681–94)

We are moved to warn ourselves against any final interpretation which tries to deny the seriousness and power of these lines and of the hymns which open and close Book III, yet nonetheless we go on—not knowing whether consistency is possible—to see that, as the meanings adjust and readjust themselves, the third stage does occur: we come around again to agree with Criseyde's denial of true happiness. One of the main elements that produces this response is the wry comedy throughout, and especially the fairly broad comedy in Book III.[10] Their happy love there is put in a comic perspective that forces us to see it from a detached point of view. Chaucer leads us to the lofty consummation by a path that emphasizes the ridiculous and even trivial details of physical indignity and psychological frailty. By increasing thus, with the addition of a comic point of view, the size and complexity of the world rendered, Chaucer diminishes the stature of what he portrays: at Criseyde's loving reproach Troilus faints; while he is unconscious, she and Pandarus undress him and put him to bed with her; and as they rub his wrists, he is shocked and frightened to wake up in circumstances supposed to be blissful. In addition to this slapstick there is a strong sense of Pandarus' presence to heighten our awareness of ourselves as spectators. Significantly, these distancing elements—physical comedy, ironic lines, and the sense of Pandarus' presence—are not in Boccaccio.

Though comedy brings a detached point of view, we probably

10. The extent of the comedy is sometimes underemphasized. Muscatine does it justice in a passage specifically exploring its effects. *Chaucer and the French Tradition,* pp. 153 ff.

would not see in it a denial of worldly happiness were it not echoed and pointed by the ending of the poem. The comic detachment in the poem leads to and is made to culminate in the theme at the end of looking down clearly from a great distance. Troilus looks down from the eighth sphere and "laughs in himself" just as we and Pandarus had many times "laughed inwardly" at the lovers. Such laughter constitutes in itself a kind of looking down. That we should be made to smile at the efforts of the lovers to bring each other to bliss means that we are being made to feel the limits of such happiness—to see it as circumscribed: to "avyse/ This litel spot of erthe, that with the se/ Embraced is" (V, 1815-17).

In fact, the poem's disputed ending ties together our final assent to both of the speeches we have been examining. The key is the contrast between the image of Troilus in the eighth sphere looking down and laughing, and that of those below who are blind and who weep. We have already noted some implied connection between determinism and a detached view that sees clearly from a distance. Troilus' whole argument for determinism involves God's seeing, and, in particular, His seeing the far-off end. Fortune, too, is recurringly conceived of as looking down and smiling, laughing, or making faces. She catches and blinds poor fools (IV, 5). And to understand Fortune involves seeing the world clearly.[11] On two occasions, Pandarus stands with Troilus on the top of the wall looking down across the plains:

11. But forth hire cours Fortune ay gan to holde:
       Criseyde loveth the sone of Tideus,
       And Troilus moot wepe in cares colde.
       Swich is this world, whoso it can byholde. (V, 1745-48)

the first time he laughs quietly to himself at Troilus' eagerness; the second time he clearly sees as a cart coming across the plains what Troilus had mistaken for Criseyde (V, 1162).

On the other hand, blindness, as the previous example illustrates so vividly, is the inability to see the end ("fyn") or what is far-off. And to weep is to think that happiness is possible. Troilus and Criseyde are blinded by love. This is true on the level of courtly imagery, and on a deeper level as well. Criseyde was blind to the "end," for she recurrently asked what was the "end" of her life, or what was the "end" of Troilus' and Pandarus' intentions (II, 424–25, 757; III, 124–26). The poem constantly refers to the "end" of love, bliss, as being carried to heaven.[12] The splendid rhetoric of the ending joins with the imagery to tie together these themes:

> Swich fyn hath, lo, this Troilus for love!
> Swich fyn hath al his grete worthynesse!
> Swich fyn hath his estat real above,
> Swich fyn his lust, swich fyn hath his noblesse!
> Swich fyn hath false worldes brotelnesse! (V, 1828–32)

III

We have seen that the ending is particularly important in contributing to our third response in which we agree again with the detached point of view expressed in the speeches. It would seem that the poem at last affirms definitely that true freedom and true happiness are not possible on earth. And yet many readers testify to the peculiarly Chaucerian effect whereby the poem seems finally to affirm both a detached and an involved point of view,

12. See, for example, I, 41, 623; III, 342, 704, 1251, 1271, 1322, 1657.

which in this case would involve both agreement and disagreement with the speeches. We can finish by trying to explain how this happens.

But first: to a reader who feels simply that the poem affirms only one point of view, my attempts to explain *how* it affirms two are not likely to be persuasive. Only appreciative, impressionistic criticism can really change a reader's response. Nonetheless, I would point to three aspects of the poem which do seem to indicate that it somehow continues to deny the speeches in spite of our third, affirmative response:

1) In the end we feel that Criseyde is guilty in some important respect, and this is strong evidence that we are left still believing in the reality of human freedom in the poem. Though we accept the speaker's hedging about her guilt because we see the respects in which all is necessary, yet we feel it is right that he never actually denies her guilt, for there is freedom too.

2) If we explore the difference between our point of view and the points of view of both Pandarus and the narrator, we see another illustration of how we have been led to be both detached and involved. We do not simply see the events through the naïve and pious eyes of the narrator; the ironic point of view of Pandarus keeps us from doing so. But on the other hand it is not long before we see the limitation of the view from inside Pandarus' head: the presence and the technique of the narrator teach us greater naïveté and innocence than Pandarus has. We are better able than he is to involve ourselves and participate in the love and joy.

3) Even though the detached themes of the ending—looking down and laughing—reinforce, as we have seen, the detached

sentiments of the speeches, nonetheless they do so in a paradoxical way that keeps alive our denial of the speeches. Throughout the poem we thought we were comfortably able to take a detached view of these affairs; so often we could look down and smile understandingly on the actors. But the ending turns the tables, and Troilus has the laugh on us. The additional distance and perspective he has in looking down on us are as great as ours had been in looking down on his dismay when he found himself in bed with Criseyde. The ending carries detachment beyond mortality where we cannot follow. We understand the ending perfectly well, and may even feel vicariously what it says; yet still we are left weeping below.

In trying to understand Chaucerian irony, or his gift for having it both ways, we could simply say, on the basis of what we have already done, that he renders the events from two vantage points instead of just one; and that they seem to supplement each other: Chaucer can show us how love looks from a distance without needing to deny the way it looks from close up. We have hinted as much in our remarks about his characterization of Criseyde and his narrative technique. With respect to his characterization of Criseyde, we have seen a sense of unfreedom when she is with Diomede which modifies the earlier sense of freedom in her behavior with Troilus. But on the other hand, the intimate rendering of her affair with Troilus makes us see the inadequacy of merely calling her passive and unfree in her affair with Diomede, and we read in elements of agency and control she exercised earlier. With respect to narrative technique, the sense of determinism in the detachment of Books IV and V reflects back upon the first half of the poem. Yet because Chaucer so often alludes concurrently to fortune in the first half, he conditions us to be aware of activity and agency—even comedy—behind the broad strokes of fortune emphasized by the astringent technique of the last two books. Thus, although the detached point of view may be more lasting and generalizable, we see it is not therefore more true than an involved point of view from close up.

As long as we keep to these terms—how behavior has free and unfree elements, and how love looks from near and far—we understand Chaucer's achievement as the portrayal of the complexity of life as it is perceived and experienced: that is, his use of language for narrative and lyric purposes impresses us more for its conformity to the way things are (good mimesis), than for its violation of the way we understand or conceptualize things (bad logic). But because he is interested in philosophical questions, Chaucer conceives in the philosopher's terms the "problem of freedom" and the "problem of happiness." The two Boethian speeches are the most striking of the many uses of language in the poem that prevent us from responding only on the narrative and lyric level: our philosophical expectations have been aroused and we want to know with our intellects whether or not men can be free and happy. Hence, in order to achieve the rich accuracy of mimesis, he has to succeed in violating the laws of discursive language and logic; that is, he must succeed in affirming that men both can and also cannot be truly free and happy.

It is by means of poetry that generates the three responses explored here that Chaucer preserves opposite assertions from their normal fate of being undermined by each other. The trick lies in the fact that something will only stay said if it is said in the full light of its opposite. This is the method of simple irony which uses its opposite to express its meaning. Ironic statements are thus difficult to deny or ridicule. Accordingly, in order to affirm seriously not only that all is determined and sad, but also that there is freedom and happiness, Chaucer makes both assertions ironically. He affirms each through the denial of its contrary. But for this really to work, the contrary must in each case be there first: that is why there must be three steps and not two. We must say yes before our no is valid; but the yes is not effective till the third step when it is said over against the no; still, the final yes does not undermine the previous no because statements cannot be canceled out which are thus made in full light of their opposite. In other words, our denial of the speeches comes only after we have sensed some truth to them; and our final agreement comes only after truly seeing—such that we cannot give it up—that they work ironically.

Good readers of Chaucer warn against reading him as more openly funny or cute than he is. Though we intuitively recognize the distortion when someone else makes it, it is an easy one to fall into. We can now more precisely see why. For the building block of Chaucer's method is the creation of simple irony: serious statement which the context ridicules. But by compounding this simple irony with another upon it, he radically deepens the quality of the response to the whole. Out of ironic steps, at times even puckish ones, he builds a final serious response. And so we see why the characteristic effect of Chaucer's best poetry is not broadly funny, even though comedy plays such a large role; and why he is not negative in his irony, nor finally sentimental in his affirmativeness. For by creating the three responses, Chaucer affirms both positions and denies nothing. Yet he is clear-sighted, unsentimental, and precise because he only affirms ironically.

Autobiography and Art:
An Elizabethan Borderland
❖ ❖ ❖

RUDOLF GOTTFRIED

THE VALIDITY of a historical approach to literature turns, I believe, on the nature of the understanding in question. Those who
seriously attempt to define literary criticism today seem to be in
general agreement that its primary aim is understanding, rather
than appreciation or evaluation; but there is no general agreement on the relationship of literary understanding to the kind of
understanding which is based on historical knowledge. Do they
represent two autonomous and metaphysically separate fields of
study, as some critics have supposed; or are they contiguous and
sometimes interdependent species of insight deriving from similar faculties of mind?

The question embraces far too much, of course, to be answered
merely on the basis of a single type of historical evidence such as
literary biography; indeed, my present subject includes only a
small subdivision of that subdivision of the evidence. Nevertheless, in discussing the autobiographical element in Elizabethan
literature, one is inevitably committed to a point of view on the
relevance of historical understanding to the literary works with
which he deals. A work of art, I assume, therefore, is never altogether free of external circumstances, whether directly concerned with the artist or otherwise. It does not exist in separation

from historical reality; it exists at the border, at the point where reality stops. And from the partial continuity of art with real experience it is a fair, though hardly a profound, deduction that any adjacent element of that experience may be of value for understanding a work of art. Thus, biographical material is one of many potential factors in literary criticism, factors, I believe, whose interrelationships and relative importance are bound to vary from work to work, from author to author, and, perhaps most of all, from period to period.

If these assumptions underlie my view of Elizabethan auto-biography, I hope they will also justify a brief excursion into that field. Autobiography in the strictly modern sense, to be sure, hardly exists for Elizabethan literature, and the single bona fide example of it which has survived is not, as we shall see in a moment, very fully developed; my concern, therefore, is chiefly with a small body of works, most of them poems, which are only in part or obliquely autobiographical. This curious choice of sub-ject, however, has certain advantages. For one thing, it reduces the amount to be covered (an absolute advantage for a lazy scholar), and reduces it to a kind of literary material in which the biographical intent is relatively clear, at least for this period, since any writer who exploits his own life must do so deliber-ately. At the same time, the dilution of autobiography with other elements, due though it be in part to the undeveloped state of the genre, has the peculiar advantage of focusing attention on the borderline between life and art, and of suggesting how the Elizabethan writer himself may have viewed their relationship. It may even suggest an Elizabethan solution to the problem which biography is bound to pose for literary criticism.

The prose account of his own life which the musician Thomas Whythorne composed about 1576 is probably the earliest English autobiography in the modern sense of the term: an honor for which it qualifies, as its editor has shown, because it is the earliest sustained history of an Englishman's life, written in the first person with a conscious attempt at literary form.[1] Whythorne, moreover, had no real model for an autobiography of this kind. The numerous lives of kings and saints available to him, aside from the fact that they were written in the third person, were not patterns for describing the humble affairs of an Elizabethan music-master; and there is no evidence that he knew Augustine's *Confessions* or the autobiographies, still in manuscript, of Cardan and Cellini.[2] He addresses his life to a friend, unnamed, who had already given the writer an oral account of himself; Whythorne had no other audience, if indeed his friend can be called one. And with this lack of literary context goes an innate timidity which is the keynote of his personality: he seems to have spent most of his youth eluding the advances of the ladies who employed him; when one of them began to grow too warm, he would tell her, to quote his own words, "I must confess that I loved her as much as I might do with a safe conscience."[3] But if he occasionally succeeds in investing himself with the aura of an Elizabethan Joseph Andrews, this is hardly a sophisticated literary achievement. At every turn the limitations of his mentality and understanding emerge in moral clichés, and the structure he endeavors to read into his life is merely the Renaissance

---

1. James M. Osborn, *The Beginnings of Autobiography in England* (Los Angeles, 1960), pp. 3–4; see also Thomas Whythorne, *The Autobiography,* ed. James M. Osborn (Oxford, 1961), Introduction, *passim.*
  2. Whythorne, *Autobiography,* p. lviii.   3. *Ibid.,* p. 113.

commonplace on the Ages of Man: whether there are three or more of them he fails to decide.[4] In other words, the first English autobiography is not a work of any intellectual boldness or depth; it is original by accident.

Nevertheless, as Mr. Osborn has noted, Whythorne uses a device which has a special interest for us: about a quarter of his book consists of poems he wrote at various times, and in the prose surrounding them he frequently explains the circumstances under which they were written.[5] Thus his life becomes, for the moment, a kind of running commentary on the poem it spawned, with an effect which is unusual in the sixteenth century. He tells us, for example, how a wealthy widow he was tutoring courted him with presents of cloth and money which he gratefully accepted:

To show myself very glad of that friendship which I received, and the rather in hope of that which was like to come after that which was past, I, seeming to rejoice before the conquest was won, made this that followeth:

> Since I embrace my lady's grace in sort as I desire,
> I will rejoice with pleasant voice since quenchèd is this fire.
> Was never none did sigh and moan more oft than I ere this
> When looks awry I did espy in the eyes of my bliss;
> But with mine eyes which be my spies I now spy thine eyes' shine,
> That once did wrest my joy t'unrest and all my mirth untwine.
> Wherefore rejoice, both sound and voice; let no tune mourning be,
> But with delight with all your might rejoice with heart and me.

Whereas before I spake of the quenching of fire, understand no otherwise thereof but only the obtaining of my desire of the benefits that I received at her hands; also, whereas you and such other sus-

4. *Ibid.,* pp. lix, 1.   5. *Ibid.,* p. lv.

picious heads would think peradventure that so much friendship as
I spake of in the foresaid song could not be except a conjunction
copulative had been made sometimes for a confirmation of the same,
to the which I must say, and say truly, that neither my hand nor any
other part of mine did once touch that part of hers where the conjunction is made. Marry, thus much may I say, that I being loth that
she should withdraw her good will from me, was very serviceable to
please her, and also would sometimes be pleasant and merry and also
somewhat bold with her, after the which times she would sometimes
tell me in scoffing manner that I was but a hoddypeak and lacked
audacity.[6]

In view of this passage it may be too audacious to compare
Whythorne's technique of commenting on his own poem with
Dante's in the *Vita Nuova;* and Mr. Osborn is inclined to doubt
that George Gascoigne's use of a similar technique in *The
Adventures of Master F. J.* had any influence on Whythorne.[7]
But quite apart from sources and analogues, such a passage
serves to illuminate a large body of Elizabethan poetry in a remarkable way. The song "Since I embrace my lady's grace" is a
characteristic love lyric of the period, so conventional in sentiment and imagery that it is hard to distinguish it from a hundred others or to believe that Whythorne himself regarded it as
more than a frigid exercise. Yet his commentary on it is doubly
significant: on the one hand he discloses that "suspicious heads"
like his friend will find a specific erotic meaning in it which a
modern reader might easily overlook without this help; on the
other, the poet himself reveals that when he wrote he had in
mind, not this erotic meaning, but his equally specific love of the
lady's gifts. In either case, it is clear that for the Elizabethan

6. *Ibid.*, pp. 42–43.   7. *Ibid.*, pp. liv–lv.

reader precise biographical circumstances underlay a poem which seems to be only a stereotyped verbal structure: it is a coin, a conventional token, which at one time bought real goods. And our awareness that this poem has little intrinsic value does not lessen the probability that under their conventional exterior many far better Elizabethan poems harbor biographical allusions which were once important to their authors.

The probability is strengthened by *The Adventures of Master F. J.,* whether or not Whythorne was influenced by the publication of this prose tale in 1573. Its autobiographical character, to be sure, has been denied on the ground that Gascoigne displays the subtlety and skill of a creative artist in telling it.[8] One may challenge the logic which assumes that sophisticated literary art is somehow incompatible with the use of material drawn from the author's own life; but for our purpose it is unimportant whether or not *Master F. J.* is in fact autobiographical. The important thing is that Gascoigne constantly implies its dependence on an actual situation and that his contemporaries must have read it as a *roman à clef* since, in order to meet the charge that he had libeled real people, he later made extensive changes which give it the air of being merely a translation from the Italian. Thus, like Whythorne's autobiography, though with far more self-consciousness, it straddles the border between reality and art.

Furthermore, Gascoigne, like Whythorne, uses a series of poems around which much of his prose narrative is developed in the form of a commentary. This device is peculiarly well fitted to the comic approach which G. T., the fictitious narrator, takes to the love affair between the wife of a country gentleman and her

8. Robert P. Adams, "Gascoigne's 'Master F.J.' as Original Fiction," *PMLA,* LXXIII (1958), 315–26.

young guest F. J., who may qualify as a kind of Elizabethan Tom Jones. At one point the narrator remarks with ironic casualness:

Well, I dwell too long upon these particular points in discoursing this trifling history, but that the same is the more apt mean of introduction to the verses which I mean to reherse unto you, and I think you will not disdain to read my conceit with his inventions about declaration of his comedy. The next that ever F. J. wrote then, upon any adventure happened between him and this fair lady, was this, as I have heard him say, and upon this occasion. After he grew more bold and better acquainted with his mistress's disposition, he adventured one Friday in the morning to go unto her chamber, and thereupon wrote as followeth, which he termed a Friday's breakfast:

> That selfsame day, and of that day that hour
> When she doth reign that mocked Vulcan the smith
> And thought it meet to harbor in her bower
> Some gallant guest for her to dally with:
> That blessèd hour, that blessed and happy day,
> I thought it meet with hasty steps to go
> Unto the lodge wherein my lady lay,
> To laugh for joy or else to weep for woe.
> And lo, my lady of her wonted grace
> First lent her lips to me, as for a kiss,
> And after that her body to embrace,
> Wherein Dame Nature wrought no thing amiss.
> What followed next, guess you that know the trade,
> For in this sort my Friday's feast I made.

And the narrator adds, "This sonnet is short and sweet, reasonably well according to the occasion, etc." [9]

Deliberately light as the tone may be, the phrase "reasonably

9. George Gascoigne, *A Hundreth Sundrie Flowres,* ed. C. T. Prouty (Columbia, Mo., 1942), pp. 74–75.

well according to the occasion" is significant. Gascoigne establishes the topicality of the poem: it concerns what F. J. did with his hostess in her chamber on a particular day of the week, and the "real" circumstances are emphasized by the conventional allusion to Venus, the appropriately adulterous deity who also governs and in some languages gives her name to Friday. The sonnet depends for its effect on an assumed reality which lies outside itself. At the same time, as Mr. Prouty has suggested, the lines "That selfsame day, and of that day that hour" and "That blessèd hour, that blessed and happy day" seem to be a sacrilegious parody of Petrarch's famous sonnet which celebrates the beginning of his love for Laura in church on Good Friday:

> Benedetto sia 'l giorno e 'l mese e l'anno
> E la stagione e 'l tempo e l'ora e 'l punto.[10]

Clearly, Gascoigne has sewn together two disparate kinds of material, elements which he implies to be autobiographical and elements which he draws from literary tradition; and the cynical humor of the narrator serves to fuse them, as Donne's cynicism was later to fuse similar elements in his erotic lyrics.

After Gascoigne and Whythorne the technique of providing a prose account of the "real" circumstances behind a poem does not seem to have been used by any important Elizabethan writer. The impulse to give a quasi-literary form to real stories drawn from private life remained, of course, throughout the period: witness the curious little tale of his sister's resistance to seduction which Gabriel Harvey set down about 1575; witness also the autobiographical pamphlets of Robert Greene and the anony-

10. *Canzoniere*, No. 61. See Prouty in Gascoigne, *Hundreth Sundrie Flowres*, p. 250.

mous *Willobie His Avisa,* published in 1594, that prosaic versification of an actual case in which the chastity of an innkeeper's wife triumphed over her suitors. But the significance of the commentaries furnished by Whythorne and Gascoigne appears on the larger stage of Elizabethan poetry, and particularly in the established genres of the sonnet sequence and the pastoral.

The sophisticated poetry of any period is colored, to some extent, with a developed self-consciousness; it may therefore, under the right conditions, take a turn in the direction of autobiography, which is a natural outgrowth of a poet's concern with himself. And there is no better illustration of this tendency than the first of all sonnet sequences, founded as it is on the rock, or rather abyss, of Petrarch's self-consciousness. The poet's use of autobiographical fact—in the exact dating, for example, of the moment when his love began and of the day on which Laura died—seems to be so normal a consequence of his feelings that we overlook the novel effect it must have had on contemporaries whose literary expectations were less fully developed than ours. Indeed, when the backwash of Petrarchanism set in, a century after the *Canzoniere* was completed, it surprises us that the elements in his poetry which were most concrete and psychologically vivid should have been reduced, by even the best of his Continental imitators, to literary formulas, apparently without personal meaning. If they recognized the original effectiveness of those elements, they killed it by endlessly transcribing rather than re-creating them.

But the history of Elizabethan sonnet sequences from Sidney to Drayton marks a genuine though momentary revival of the genre. In the 1590s, it goes without saying, English poets were quite as imitative as any of their Continental brethren, many of them as slavishly imitative as the worst of the Petrarchisti. Nevertheless, the Elizabethan sonneteer enjoyed the paradoxical advantage of imitating poems which were already imitations: for him the obsessive hold of Petrarch's techniques was usually weakened by transmission through Italian and French paraphrases, so that his own qualities, for better or worse, had an opportunity to mingle somewhat more fully with the borrowed conventions. Partly as a result of this, the poorer sequences are at times characterized by an incredible mawkishness, often coupled with a radical breakdown of sense and meter. On the other hand, three or four of the best sonneteers reveal an independence in both the choice and the treatment of their subjects which is equally unorthodox.

Sidney's *Astrophel and Stella,* the bellwether of the English sonnet sequences, announces the poet's independence in the most explicit terms. He constantly asserts that, since he writes from the heart, he is uncontaminated by any literary fashion, Petrarchan or otherwise; and if a modern reader is inclined to set much of this down to mere bravado, given Sidney's frequent use of Petrarchan conventions and the Petrarchan nature of his frustrated love for a married woman, still the poet describes that love with a humor, pathos, and dramatic liveliness which give the whole work an unusual air of freshness and actuality. *Astrophel and Stella,* indeed, is compact of material drawn directly from Sidney's life, beginning with his own identification of Stella as Penelope Rich, née Devereux: an exploitation of reality which goes far beyond anything that Petrarch tells us about Laura. On occasion he includes autobiographical allusions which are almost self-explanatory, as though he made the poems themselves provide what Whythorne and Gascoigne had left to their prose commentaries; but the depth of his autobiographical commitment is also revealed by other allusions which time has hidden from later readers. To cite an example which is not perhaps so insignificant as it may seem, he gives both Stella and Astrophel, in separate sonnets, their armorial bearings:

> Cupid then smiles, for on his crest there lies
> Stella's fair hair; her face he makes his shield
> Where roses gules are borne in silver field.

Under this conventional description, as no Elizabethan needed to be told, the poet refers directly to the Devereux coat of arms, three disks, suggesting roses, which are gules, or red, on a silver field. Later he addresses the same god of love to similar effect:

> Yet let this thought thy tigrish courage pass,
> That I perhaps am somewhat kin to thee
> Since in thine arms, if learn'd fame truth hath spred,
> Thou bear'st the arrow, I the arrow head.

Here the hackneyed quip on Cupid's arrow conceals an allusion to the Sidney coat of arms, which bears a pheon, or arrowhead.[11] The witty use of such small autobiographical facts, even when they are recognized, may easily be dismissed as mere Alexandrian ingenuity; but their cumulative effect is also important for the critic. They reinforce our sense that *Astrophel and Stella*, whatever it owes to various literary traditions, is never out of contact

11. Sonnets 13 and 65. See William Ringler's edition of *The Poems of Sir Philip Sidney* (Oxford, 1962), pp. 465–66, 479.

with reality; and specifically, in these heraldic details, they emphasize the patrician strain which runs through Sidney's art.

Moreover, his successors tend to preserve some of Sidney's concreteness in dealing with their own less aristocratic lives. The sonneteers of the 1590s not only plagiarize his phrases and in various ways reassert his independence from Petrarchan formulas; they also tie their sentiments to specific circumstances which have the appearance of reality. Daniel, a devoted follower of Sidney, is a case in point. His *Delia,* which is surely one of the most conventional Elizabethan sequences, may very well describe an imaginary love affair; but the textual evidence for this also reveals a continued desire to give his work an air of autobiographical truth. For example, he tells us in one sonnet that Delia dashed his love *three* years after it began; in a later version he raises the number to *five,* which, if more euphonious, is equally concrete. At another place he outrageously alters the color of her hair from *golden* to *sable,* which is more suitable to the context; but again, there has been no loss in the reality implied.[12] If Daniel's love is probably a literary fiction from start to finish, he nevertheless considers it effective to maintain, even in minute details, the assumption that his love is circumstantially true.

The same assumption, needless to say, reinforces the effect of Shakespeare's sonnets, where much of the poet's material, unlike Daniel's, must be autobiographical in fact. He plays the realistic portrait of his dark mistress off against the traditional blond angel; or to take less obvious cases, he associates his feelings for

12. Sonnets 26 and 34. See Arthur C. Sprague's edition of Daniel's *Poems and a Defence of Rime* (Cambridge, Mass., 1930), pp. 179, 185.

her with her performance on the virginals and his feelings for his friend with a journey on horseback.[13] For all his reputed impersonality, Shakespeare exploits his personal life on every level of the sonnets, from literal description to complicated metaphor; and this not merely in defiance of Petrarchanism, but also in conformity with the prevailing habit of the Elizabethan sequences.

In the Elizabethan period, of course, the bent toward autobiographical concreteness is not limited to the sonnet: it appears in many separate lyrics and in that curious collection of related love poems which Ralegh addressed to the Queen under the title of *The Ocean to Cynthia,* cloudy as its allusions are to his life at court.[14] But the down-to-earth interest in themselves which, as we have seen, was already becoming a characteristic of English poets must have been fostered by the challenge of the sonnet sequence. With its panoply of formal conventions and its autobiographical implications, it was a medium peculiarly fitted for attempting to bring reality into relation with art; and the better sonneteers are all to some extent concerned with this relationship. None of those already named, however, not even Sidney or Shakespeare, explores it more freely than Spenser does.

At a first reading his *Amoretti* has the appearance of being the least original of Elizabethan sequences. Spenser, unlike Sidney, makes no overt claim to have broken with literary tradition; he has none of Shakespeare's sensational subject matter. A few of his sonnets, especially those near the beginning, paraphrase Continental poets; many of them reflect such Petrarchan stereotypes

13. Sonnets 127, 130, 128, 50.

14. On the background and collective structure of this work see Walter Oakshott, *The Queen and the Poet* (London, 1960).

as "My loue is lyke to yse, and I to fyre." [15] At the same time, their even, unemphatic tone has led some foreign critics to call them frigid and passionless: an effect perhaps due in part to Spenser's interlocking rhyme scheme, which favors continuity and overrides dramatic reversals within the structure of the sonnet. [16] Moreover, the parting of the lovers at the end of the sequence inevitably reminds us of the unhappy outcome expected of any normal Petrarchan attachment.

And yet, in its own unobtrusive way, the *Amoretti* is one of the most original of Elizabethan literary works. If the lovers are parted at the end of it, they are married in its sequel; and this in spite of the traditional point of view which must have found it almost more unorthodox to resolve a sonnet sequence in an epithalamion than to make it express, as Shakespeare does, the frustrations of a love divided between man and woman. Not only is Spenser's *Epithalamion* a poem of great originality in its own right, but it also illuminates the marriage theme which underlies the conventional surface of the *Amoretti*. There, it reveals, the poet intends from the first "to knit the knot, that euer shall remaine"; [17] and the lady's acceptance of his suit, nearly three quarters of the way through, not only becomes the pivot of the narrative structure but marks an all-important if subtle turning point in the emotional tone of the whole. As soon as she has become his fiancée, the poet begins to write with an intimacy,

15. Sonnet 30.

16. See Peter Borghesi and Emile Legouis in the Variorum Edition of *The Works of Edmund Spenser* (Baltimore, 1932–57), VIII, 629–30; also J. W. Lever, *The Elizabethan Love Sonnet* (London, 1956), pp. 130 ff.

17. Sonnet 6.

and at times a sensuality, which he has never allowed himself to express before.[18] Throughout much of the sequence, moreover, what may be called the seriousness of his intentions accounts for a kind of playful humor which Mr. Martz has acutely diagnosed.[19] Only a lover with a good conscience, one who intended to marry her, would ever address his mistress with Spenser's gentle irony:

> When my abodes prefixed time is spent,
> My cruell fayre streight bids me wend my way:
> but then from heauen most hideous stormes are sent
> as willing me against her will to stay.
> Whom then shall I or heauen or her obay?
> the heauens know best what is the best for me:
> but as she will, whose will my life doth sway,
> my lower heauen, so it perforce must bee.
> But ye high heuens, that all this sorowe see,
> sith all your tempests cannot hold me backe:
> aswage your stormes, or else both you and she,
> will both together me too sorely wrack.
> Enough it is for one man to sustaine
> the stormes, which she alone on me doth raine.[20]

Submission to the cruel fair who, on a stormy night, requires the poet to leave at his prefixed time may be a discreet attempt to parody the cruelty of a Petrarchan mistress; what is more to the point, the concreteness and self-assurance of Spenser's drollery

18. The turning point occurs in Sonnet 63; for the consequences see sonnets 64, 76, 77.

19. Louis L. Martz, "The *Amoretti:* 'Most Goodly Temperature,'" in *Form and Convention in the Poetry of Edmund Spenser,* ed. William Nelson (New York, 1961), pp. 146–68.

20. Sonnet 46.

have every appearance of referring to a real episode. This sonnet must have been written after an actual meeting between lovers who were already on the way to married intimacy.

Throughout the *Amoretti,* indeed, the problem of Spenser's originality as an artist is very closely allied to his use of autobiographical material. The sequence presumably tells the story of how he wooed and won the mistress whom he marries, as we have seen, in the *Epithalamion;* she is clearly intended to be Elizabeth Boyle, his second wife, and from his deliberate references to days and seasons we may infer that he must have begun his suit late in 1592, when he was about forty, that she must have accepted him early in 1594, and that they must have been married on June 11 of that year.[21] Moreover, the intimate tone and circumstantial evidence of many passages support the plausibility of the poet's account. Nevertheless, it has long been suspected that some of the earlier *Amoretti* were written to another woman than his second wife, perhaps to Lady Elizabeth Carey; and Mr. Lever has offered to identify no less than eighteen of the intruded sonnets.[22] Spenser, if we are to believe this, is nearly as adroit as Laurence Sterne, who sent the same love letter to his wife and later to another woman. But here the poet's callousness serves a larger purpose: he is using extraneous material to enrich the aesthetic appeal of a narrative which is undoubtedly autobiographical in its main outlines, and it is significant that the sonnets which he may have inserted among those actually written in honor of Elizabeth Boyle are more conventional than

21. Sonnets 4, 19, 22, 60, 68; *Epithalamion,* ll. 265–66.
22. See Variorum Edition, VIII, 634–38; Lever, *Elizabethan Love Sonnet,* p. 102.

most of the others. In the same way, the separation of the lovers, whether or not it can be explained in terms of a temporary separation of the real couple, is given an artificial importance by being placed at the end of the sequence, where it traditionally belongs.[23] Evidence of Spenser's continuing desire to bring his original material into a more perfect form may even be detected in the puzzling repetition of sonnet 35 as sonnet 83: at the last moment, in Ireland, he perhaps marked it for transfer from one position to another; but his publisher, in London, misunderstanding the manuscript, had the poem printed in both positions —a blunder which, if I am right, betrays the poet in the act of correction.

At any rate, the *Amoretti* is an outstanding case of the Elizabethan tendency to reorganize and adapt autobiography to external considerations. More than any of his contemporaries in this genre, Spenser consciously doubles back and forth across the border between reality and art, tangling and untangling their relationship with a kind of creative playfulness.

When the *Amoretti* was written, in fact, no other Elizabethan poet had become quite so adept as Spenser was at violating borders. By its very nature allegorical writing draws upon the relationships between different levels of experience; but in *The Faerie Queene,* on which he worked throughout his maturity, the simple one-to-one equivalents of standard allegory had evolved into a complex technique of shifting, interwoven meanings which still defeats schematic criticism. The literal narrative represents not only moral relations in general but political history in

23. See Martz, in *Form and Convention,* pp. 148–50.

particular, not only abstract ideas but real persons, not only
public but private realities. On various occasions the same character may represent different ideas or different persons, and
different characters may represent the same idea or the same
person. Furthermore, the narrative is not always allegorical; and
in at least one episode an unallegorical character is transformed
into allegory before our eyes. Indeed, though Fairyland is the
country in which the whole story presumably takes place, it has
never been easy to determine its meaning or its boundaries: does
it face our world across the Severn or across the River of Ocean?
Spenser teases us by suggesting that it will eventually be discovered like Virginia or Peru.[24] Yet in the meantime the inhabi-
tants of Britain and Fairyland are mingled in his poem as if there
were no difference in the breeds nor any formalities to hinder
them from passing and repassing that invisible border. Thus,
whenever we try to pin down too much of it, the allegory of *The
Faerie Queene* eludes us.

This must be partly due to the piecemeal fashion in which *The
Faerie Queene* itself was composed; at the same time, however, it
reveals a general cast or habit of mind, fostered and exercised in
writing allegory, but also at work in poems which Spenser wrote
with little or no allegorical intention. For him poetry as such, in
several of its forms, had come to provide a release from established limits; it had become a passport to move freely among the
various realms of experience, crossing their boundaries at will,
with all the happy self-assurance of his own hero, Clarion the
butterfly. In particular, as we have seen, this disposition to exploit
borders fastened on the sonnet sequence; and in the end it turned

24. *FQ*, 2. pr. 2.

even more boldly to the autobiographical implications of another genre.

When *The Shepheardes Calender* was published in 1579, pastoral poetry had already had a long and complicated history, running its course through several European literatures; in English, however, it was a comparative newcomer, hitherto represented only by recent and rather feeble examples. Accordingly, Spenser was intent not so much on developing the genre in new directions as in showing that all of its traditional features could be brilliantly realized in English and on English themes. He made *The Shepheardes Calender* a source book of verse forms and within the annual cycle accepted a division of his eclogues by conventional type. If many of them, as Mr. McLane has proved, reveal the young poet's intense concern for the political and religious issues of the time, it is coupled with an emphasis on literary workmanship which seems to have made the strongest impression on his contemporaries.[25] Thus the volume is for the most part experimental in the limited field of technique rather than original, like the *Amoretti* and *The Faerie Queene,* in the free adaptation of experience to poetry.

The truth of this is clearly demonstrated by the autobiographical elements in the *Calender.* On the model of Vergil it had long been customary for pastoral poets to introduce themselves among their shepherds; and with a nod to the "Romish *Tityrus,*" Spenser deliberately sets forth, or pretends to set forth, his real feelings and affairs in the person of Colin Clout.[26]

25. Paul E. McLane, *Spenser's Shepheardes Calender* (Notre Dame, 1961), *passim;* for contemporary reactions see Variorum Edition, VII, 571–72.

26. Variorum Edition, VII, 10, 93.

Through his hero he apparently allows us to learn something about his own literary ambitions; but it is curious that, while Colin is assigned the three lyrics of which their real author was probably most proud, he does not represent Spenser when Spenser's career as a poet is fully and explicitly discussed by less important characters in the October eclogue. Colin serves, primarily, to represent him in the role of the traditional unhappy lover of Renaissance pastoral. His luckless passion for Rosalind is frustrated by her coldness throughout the *Calender;* at one point she submits to the treachery of a rival named Menalcas; and at the same time Colin is assailed with good advice by Hobbinol, his well-intentioned if slightly jealous friend. The whole situation—it can hardly be called a story—remains conventionally static and undeveloped.

Nevertheless, the situation must be founded, to a considerable extent, on reality. Menalcas is too shadowy to be unmasked, at least without more evidence than we now have; but if Colin is specifically identified by the original editor as the poet himself, Hobbinol is also specifically identified as Gabriel Harvey, who was Spenser's most intimate friend at the time.[27] In fact, Harvey's rather crusty personality occasionally shows through in Hobbinol, with convincing verisimilitude. Rosalind, on the other hand, is characterized only by her coldness and, in the text of the poem, is identified only as "the Widdowes daughter of the glenne."[28] With no more to go on, one might almost, in despera-

27. *Ibid.,* VII, 93.

28. "Aprill," l. 26. E.K., the editor, adds that "shee is a Gentle woman of no meane house, nor endewed with anye vulgare and common gifts both of nature and manners" (Variorum Edition, VII, 42); on the other hand, Spenser himself, writing to Harvey in 1579, calls her "a priuate Personage vnknowne" (*ibid.,* IX, 5).

tion, accept the possibility for which Mr. McLane has so inge-
niously argued, that she is Queen Elizabeth.[29] But fortunately
Harvey, writing to the poet himself in the spring of 1580, refers
to *"Colina Clouta,"* that is Spenser's wife, probably née Mach-
abyas Childe, as *"Rosalindula,"* Little Rosalind: Harvey's Latin
phrase has been variously translated, but the context, I think,
makes this identification inescapable.[30] Thus, three of the four
actors in the private drama of Colin's love can be matched with
real persons.

Spenser's procedure has been remarkable, to say the least. He
has chosen to represent a situation from his own life, the love
affair which culminated in his first marriage, probably some
months before the publication of his book; but in the eclogues,
where the conventions of the genre resisted such an outcome, the
poet's love is doomed from first to last, from January to December. This may suggest a kind of parallel to the *Amoretti,* where
the love affair which culminated in Spenser's second marriage is
represented, at least within the sequence itself, as petering out
into a frustrating separation; in both cases an artificial element
seems to distort the reality which underlies the story. In the
Calender, however, the distortion is much greater since the poet
has more fully accepted the traditional framework of pastoral; he
only glances, here and there, at the reality and never, as in the
Amoretti, allows it to mate on equal terms with the requirements
of art. The difference is clearly revealed at the denouement of
Colin's love in the December eclogue. Here, by a tour de force
which has been much admired, Spenser contrives to present the
lover's whole life under the guise of the four seasons, which

29. McLane, *Spenser's Shepheardes Calender,* pp. 27–46.
30. Variorum Edition, IX, 476, 249; VII, 655.

parallel and summarize the cycle of the months throughout the *Calender*. But he accomplishes this technical feat at a high cost: the young poet, actually about twenty-seven years old, describes himself as being now in the winter of his age, wrinkled and white-haired; and our sense of an unnatural straining for effect is confirmed when we discover that in this passage he has borrowed the account of his happy rural youth (presumably in the heart of London) from a French pastoral by Clément Marot.[31]

Artificiality rather than boldness, then, marks his use of auto-biographical elements in *The Shepheardes Calender;* in a sense he was too timid as yet to deal directly with his own life in a poetic context; and if he had written no more pastoral poetry, there would be little reason, from our present point of view, to emphasize his contribution to that genre. But the *Calender,* like the *Amoretti,* has a sequel, albeit one composed after a significant lapse of time: in *Colin Clouts Come Home Againe,* which he drafted in 1591 and published four years later, Spenser consciously exploits and extends his earlier attempt at pastoral autobiography.

The links with the *Calender* are obvious: Colin, the central character, still represents the poet himself; Hobbinol is still a speaker in the pastoral dialogue and still the one who "lou'd this shepheard dearest in degree"; [32] and at the end of the poem a long passage is devoted to the defense of Rosalind, who is a figure of importance still. But if Spenser builds *Colin Clouts Come Home Againe* on these old foundations, the structure he now raises bears little resemblance to anything preceding it. This

31. "December," ll. 127–44, 19–36; Variorum Edition, VII, 420.
32. *CCCHA,* l. 14.

pastoral is three times as long as the longest eclogue in the *Calender;* here, in a large assembly of fellow shepherds, Colin relates a chapter of the poet's life with a circumstantial fullness which is unique in Elizabethan poetry. He tells how Ralegh, the Shepherd of the Ocean, visited him on his estate in Ireland; how each of them read a poem of his own to the other; how Ralegh persuaded his friend to go with him to England; how, after a rough crossing, they landed in a western port; how Spenser on his way up to London was enchanted with the peace and beauty of the English countryside; how the Queen overwhelmed him with her bounty; how he was filled with admiration for individual poets and ladies of the court, many of whom are praised under fictitious names; but how the general depravity of the English courtiers, their backbiting and abuse of love, finally disillusioned him before he returned to Ireland. And all this, as he asserts to Ralegh in the dedication, agrees with "the truth in circumstance and matter." In fact, it has been accepted as a fairly accurate picture of the poet's life between the autumn of 1589 and the early months of 1591.[33]

A somewhat closer examination of *Colin Clouts Come Home Againe,* however, is needed if we are to understand what Spenser means by "the truth in circumstance and matter"; for the truth which underlies the poem is curiously beset with ambiguities. The very title is calculated to tease a careful reader: is it to England or to Ireland that the poet comes home again? which is his home? and in what sense, by birth or preference? In the end I think there can be no doubt that Ireland is his home by prefer-

33. See Alexander C. Judson, *The Life of Edmund Spenser* (Baltimore, 1945), pp. 136–56.

ence; but until he attacks the court, the issue is balanced between "here" and "there." The skill with which he equivocates appears, for example, in the contrast he draws between the peacefulness of England and Ireland's disordered life:

> For there all happie peace and plenteous store
> Conspire in one to make contented blisse:
> No wayling there nor wretchednesse is heard,
> No bloodie issues nor no leprosies,
> No griesly famine, nor no raging sweard,
> No nightly bodrags, nor no hue and cries;
> The shepheards there abroad may safely lie,
> On hills and downes, withouten dread or daunger:
> No rauenous wolues the good mans hope destroy,
> Nor outlawes fell affray the forest raunger.
> There learned arts do florish in great honor,
> And Poets wits are had in peerlesse price:
> Religion hath lay powre to rest vpon her,
> Aduancing vertue and suppressing vice.

Yet in the lines that follow, the poet deliberately blurs this favorable view of England:

> For end, all good, all grace there freely growes,
> Had people grace it gratefully to vse:
> For God his gifts there plenteously bestowes
> But gracelesse men them greatly do abuse.[34]

Furthermore, the ambiguity which suspends the meaning of "home" stems from another, more fundamental quandary. It is evident from the first that Colin, a shepherd and a landsman, has never been out of Ireland before the visit to England he describes; but we know that Spenser, whom Colin represents, had

34. *CCCHA*, ll. 310–27.

come originally from England to Ireland. So, while Ireland is home for both of them in the end, it is home in a somewhat different sense, and the hero of the poem is not intended to be altogether equivalent to the poet himself. In the same way, Hobbinol is a native Irish shepherd, although Harvey, whom he represents, had never been in Ireland. Clearly, in *Colin Clouts Come Home Againe* Spenser has grafted the pastoral world of *The Shepheardes Calender* on the realities of his subsequent life. And this, it also occurs to me, may be the key to the ambiguity surrounding the figure of Rosalind. The country lass, "the Widdowes daughter of the glenne," is here transformed from a humble jilt into a lady who is noble in every sense of the term: "So hie her thoughts," Colin assures us, "as she her selfe haue place." [35] If the Rosalind of the *Calender* is actually, as we have seen, a faint conventional representation of the girl who became Spenser's first wife, who must have died in the meantime, and who had been succeeded by another wife, it would now be natural for him to erase her original identity as far as possible; and it is no less natural to do so by a kind of literary escalation which follows the same free method he uses elsewhere in dealing with autobiographical material.

During the Elizabethan period, indeed, autobiographical poetry may be said to have reached its fullest development in *Colin Clouts Come Home Againe.* For Spenser contrives to load it with more of the concrete reality of his own life than we can find in any of his other poems; at the same time, partly because it is a poem, the reality has also been carefully transposed and transformed. Thus, in the story of Mulla and Bregog which

35. *Ibid.,* l. 937.

Colin tells the Shepherd of the Ocean, the real features of the landscape around Spenser's Irish home are turned into an Ovidian myth:[36] a metamorphosis which reflects and clarifies his treatment of all the human circumstances enclosing it. Throughout the poem his imagination moves freely back and forth across the border which divides reality from art. Without confusing them or yet subordinating one to the other, he makes each of them echo and fortify the other's voice; they are mingled and contrasted in thematic counterpoint.

And this achievement, if I am right, has its wider significance. First, it is a genuine outgrowth of the Elizabethan interest in using autobiography for the substance of poetry: an interest which Spenser, with his superlative skill and intelligence, carried further than any of his contemporaries. In the second place, it suggests that, while biography as such was still too undeveloped to pose a theoretical problem for Elizabethan criticism, there was already, in practical terms, an Elizabethan solution.

36. *Ibid.*, ll. 92–155.

The Keys Are at the Palace
A Note on Criticism and Biography
❖ ❖ ❖

FRANCIS NOEL LEES

SOME YEARS ago the question of the relations of Criticism and Biography was sharply raised for the present writer by something in an essay on Rossetti by Sir Maurice Bowra. It was the following comment on one of the "House of Life" sonnets, "The Hill Summit." Sir Maurice had written as follows:

Through images [Rossetti] transforms thoughts and feelings into solid shapes. For instance, in "The Hill Summit" he tells how towards evening he climbs a hill, and this careful account of what looks like an actual occasion has a symbolical purpose. The arrival at the hill-top is his own arrival at middle age. He keeps his symbols clear and consistent and creates by visual means the atmosphere of such a situation with its imaginative appeal to him:

And now that I have climbed and won this height,
  I must tread downward through the sloping shade
And travel the bewildered tracks till night.
  Yet for this hour I still may here be stayed
And see the gold air and the silver fade
  And the last bird fly into the last light.

This is how Rossetti, at a turning-point of his life, pauses while he looks back to the past and forward to the future. The situation needs no comment from him, since it is complete in itself and belongs to common experience.[1]

1. C. M. Bowra, "The House of Life," reprinted from *The Romantic*

Read through Bowra's lens, heard through this biographical medium, the lines became deeper, more resonant, more haunting in tone, took on a more arresting significance. Read again, however, with Bowra's biographical interposition carefully held aside, this extra timbre disappeared. Clearly, there were questions to be asked.

Why did Bowra say what he had said? Did he positively know that for Rossetti the poem was not simply an observation on the pleasures and pains, the rewards, the distractions and the costs of country-walking? Was it that, from the age at which he knew Rossetti had composed the poem, the critic had deduced the necessary emergence of such a sentiment? But, as to this last conjecture, if that were indeed a general truth, did it equally follow that a hill-walk was its universal and inevitable symbol? If it were not a general truth, with what certainty could the deduction be made? It was certainly not that such a sentiment must necessarily accompany even a turning-point that was known to be one—and how many turning-points in life were recognized to be such at the time? Either Bowra was reading the poem in the context of the poet's biography (as we read, still, Nelson's "Kiss me, Hardy"—in the context of *Nelson*'s biography) or he was discerning something which was really in the poem and then adding it to the biography; and, of course, the whole cause of the questioning was the absence of anything in the lines quoted which spoke, or as good as spoke, of what it seemed exact to call a "turning-point of his life," the lack of any kind of reference to "arrival at middle age." Obviously, Bowra

Imagination (1947) in *Victorian Literature,* ed. Austin Wright (New York, 1961), p. 256.

knew from the biography what Rossetti had intended in the piece.

A reading of the complete poem did not alter this view—though it did reveal something which was later to clarify the situation and which will be mentioned in due course. The sonnet is Number XXXIII of the original "House of Life" sequence published in 1870, and must be quoted in its entirety: [2]

> This feast-day of the sun, his altar there
>   In the broad west has blazed for vesper-song;
>   And I have loitered in the vale too long
> And gaze now a belated worshipper.
> Yet may I not forget that I was 'ware,
>   So journeying, of his face at intervals
>   Transfigured where the fringed horizon falls,—
> A fiery bush with coruscating hair.
>
> And now that I have climbed and won this height,
>   I must tread downward through the sloping shade
> And travel the bewildered tracks till night.
>   Yet for this hour I still may here be stayed
>   And see the gold air and the silver fade
> And the last bird fly into the last light.

Now, what were the factors in the general question which was being raised? They seemed simple enough. The reader either added to the poem something it did not independently possess or he found in the poem something which he could add to the biog· raphy, where it might or might not find a definite counterpart. If the poem of itself conveyed what the biographical material predicted, so to put it, biography had nothing to give, it seemed; the

2. Rossetti poems here quoted from *Rossetti's Poems,* ed. Oswald Doughty (London, 1961).

meaning of the poem would have to be established, of course, before the situation could be so assessed. If, however, the poem did not find this evident match, its character would need to be precisely determined if the biographical addition was to be exact. And, in the present instance, for example, quite apart from the general theme of the poem, we should need to know whether Rossetti had written a defiant or submissive piece, a sardonic one or a sentimental one, whether he had seen things clearly, vaguely or confusedly, subtly or crudely, and so on. In either case, that was, criticism was the primary requirement, criticism unaided by biography, and not interfered with by biography.

The principles seemed to be evident, and subsequent evidence has, I believe, supported the opinion. Naturally, much depends on what is meant by "criticism"; but this is so evidently the case that really nothing substantial depends on it at all. If we wish to extend the dominion of the word, even to a total scientific and philosophical comprehensiveness, we shall then simply have to use another term for the "criticism" which is here meant, and which will be recognized by everyone, that commonplace enough undertaking to pass a judgment on something made or done or said, after having seen or heard it and understood it. And criticism, in attempting first to ascertain what has been done in and by a poem, will be judging its efficacy for the reader, and not for the poet. Words are the *result* of thought and feeling in the writer, but in the reader the *cause* of such; therefore the writer's relationship with them cannot be identical with the reader's. On the one hand, we cannot estimate the truth of Yeats's finding that he had warmed himself back into life by writing "Byzantium"; on the other, if authentic authorial motivation and intent were what provides significance and effectiveness for the reader, Mendoza's lines to his Louisa in *Man and Superman* would have to rank, we must imagine, with any greatest love-lyric we care to elect; as must also the transcription of many an actual passionate sigh or meaningful grunt—those, at any rate, of very important people.

In deciding what Rossetti says in this poem, we shall have to conclude that he indeed says nothing about a "turning-point of his life" and nothing about an "arrival at middle age"; and that what he does say is not a very close fit with what one imagines oneself feeling at any such turning-point recognized by us as such—what he says is either too much dramatized or far too tranquil. If the situation is strictly the one described, and the symbolization held to the realistic impression, then the temporary difficulty and discomfort ahead are being viewed melodramatically. If, however, the "tracks" are really "bewildered" and the night is more than the usual brief interruption of the possibilities of renewed delights (and a welcome and valuable source of refreshment after exertion), then the rest of the poem is conflictingly relishing of melancholy—a mere melancholy, it may be said. Biographical intent so specific as that proposed by Bowra cannot convincingly be ascribed to the poem; though a certain mood or frame of mind which is broadly harmonizable with the suggestion can. If we pump into the poem a little biographical air—as is likely to happen with a reader first meeting it in Bowra's essay—we may indeed increase the appeal of the piece (for some, at any rate), but we are back with Mendoza and the important person's grunt (and we shall, in fact, have gained a vague sentimental toning at the expense of a certain, admittedly unsymbolic, incisiveness). That I may have been mistaken in assuming that Bowra had simply imported, illicitly, some biographical information, it will presently appear: but this does not affect the validity of my purpose, which is to exhibit a reader taking in a poem with his mind influenced by biography, and to set forth the reasons which in this case emerged for disrecommending that process.

My attention was again drawn to the poem by Oswald Doughty's remarks in his life of Rossetti. In chronicling the history of the poet in the year 1853, he tells of the visit to Bell Scott in Newcastle some two years after the removal of Elizabeth Siddal from the milliner's shop into Rossetti's keeping. It was a time, says Doughty, when Rossetti was "baffled by both art and life"; he was "gloomily yielding to a creeping paralysis of the will"; he was "already beginning to revise his intentions of marriage." From Newcastle he returned by train to Coventry and spent some days alone in Warwickshire before returning to London. Doughty then writes as follows:

Another sonnet of this tour, *The Hill Summit,* ostensibly a poem of sunset and twilight beauty, written one evening amidst the peaceful Warwickshire scenery, is also a symbolical expression of his unrest, a record of bitterness of spirit so deep that, bidding farewell to the sun, he finally takes the downward path into a permanently darkened future. As a chance remark of Gabriel to Allingham a year later shows indeed, his mind as he wrote this sonnet was, for neither the first nor last time, turned toward suicide as a way of escape, though as yet hardly seriously. . . . His solitary pilgrimage long remained to him a gracious memory—a valediction perhaps to his earlier unfettered life.[3]

3. Oswald Doughty, *Dante Gabriel Rossetti: A Victorian Romantic* (New Haven, 1949), pp. 138–39.

This is more detailed biography than that produced by Bowra; and, Rossetti not having been born until 1828, one would not expect the poem to have been connected with his middle age— unless Bowra was working from the date of publication, 1870. The fuller statement is interesting both in what it says and how it says it.

It is noticeable that the phrase "bidding farewell to the sun, he finally takes the downward path into a permanently darkened future" goes beyond the literal statement of the poem, but seems definitely to derive from something Doughty has observed in the poem. What he has observed is, self-evidently, some exaggeration by Rossetti in respect of what would normally be of a mere few hours' duration: an impression of the poem is being incorporated in the biography, not the biographical information being injected into the poem. The event Rossetti presents is allowed to stay more distinctly in the mind of Doughty's reader as the event of hill-walking it claims to be; with the theme of time lost and of lingering in the present, to postpone and to compensate for subsequent discomfort, carrying no more than the minimal allegory implied by any such representative occurrence. When Doughty says that "his solitary pilgrimage long remained to him a gracious memory" he says no more than would acknowledge the poem to be just what it announces itself to be, and in a way which will accommodate it in the biography without necessitating any further symbolism. The phrase which follows, "a valediction perhaps to his earlier unfettered life," has its "perhaps," and refers, anyway, to the holiday not the poem. Opportunities for the reader greedy for biography, for "human interest," are present in Doughty's account, certainly, but Doughty himself does not instigate that response gratuitously, for, although, unlike

Bowra, he avowedly is acting as biographer, not as critic, he brings the poem to the biography and not vice versa. Even, I would think, when he describes the poem as "a symbolical expression of his unrest" he comes to the description by way of deduction from the poem. To discern so broad a thing as "unrest," furthermore, hardly demands the adjective "symbolical" except as merely indicating an interest in *Sinn* over and above *Bedeutung,* and as always and everywhere applicable to literature.

Later consideration has indeed produced the belief that Bowra, in private, may have worked in this order, too (his implied faulty dating suggests it), and then converted his *interpretation* into accepted biographical *information* to be reapplied to the benefit (or presumed benefit) of the poem; finding the result welcome as universal, almost archetypal, symbolism, and having none of Doughty's sense of an exaggeration on Rossetti's part in going beyond the facts presented to express feelings which could accurately be described in Doughty's phrases "bidding farewell" and "permanently darkened future."

That we cannot easily ascribe to the hilltop image a one right universal meaning of "middle age," or indeed anything chronologically or materially very specific, we are as good as warned, it then transpired, in a letter from Rossetti to his "Dear Mamma," written shortly after the return to London. He writes:

I hear you are reading Haydon's life, as I have been and am now some way through vol. iii. It gets very melancholy reading as it goes on; but altogether the book gives one a very high opinion of him, I think. I cannot see, after all, that he was so conceited as that fellow Tom Taylor wants to make out, with the insolent pity of a little snob.

He was always, or nearly so, dissatisfied with his own work, though certainly he was always saying he could see a great thing before him, which thing he really *did* see. The fact is that, when a man near the top of a hill begins going into raptures about the view his position commands, it is necessary that one should be something more than an ant even to understand him, since the ant cannot even look high enough to see that the hill is there at all.[4]

If we were to interpret the poem from *this* evidence alone, we should at any rate shift our viewpoint from the area of middle-agedness or of the domestic (e.g., to do with Elizabeth Siddal) to that of the artistic, and we should be forced to find the Bowra lead a misdirection. Bowra's biographical preamble, it becomes evident, falsifies; and so would Doughty's accompanying account, were he (or we) to let it, for despite the earlier statement that Rossetti was "baffled" by *both* art and life, he leaves active the suggestion of "his earlier unfettered life"—and the poem says nothing about "suicide" or even initial "unrest" either. Yet there is something about the poem which has worked, probably, on both Doughty and Bowra, though with different evaluational effects on each; something which, though not literally "said," is genuinely, and importantly, present in the poem. Rossetti speaks of the downward journey (is it onward or back, by the way?) with a feeling which seems to go beyond the stated facts of the situation; he articulates his statement in verse which vibrates emotionally, to suggest an inescapable hopelessness in the face of final exile into a permanent darkness. It is the movement of the verse which makes the fading of the "gold air and the silver" seem for eternity, the "last bird" and the "last light" seem

4. Oswald Doughty and John Robert Wahl, eds., *Letters of Dante Gabriel Rossetti* (Oxford, 1965), I, 149.

terminal instead of diurnal. This is a real feature of the poem itself (though one which may not operate on a superficial, a partial reading); and because no sufficient reason for it is disclosed in the poem, I myself would consider it an emotional *excess*. However much or little a reader may welcome this feature it is certainly why the poem can so easily be weighted by a plausible biographical additive and so readily acquire "human interest." Moreover, it is part of what we ultimately have to build into the biography, and to explain (if possible) from the biography; though not something to have its purport hastily predetermined. If it should be denied that this emotional feature really exists, the critical reading here put forward will be impugned, and perhaps rightly: but the principle of interpretation argued will only be given additional support—for without this emotional voicing, there is no warrant for talk of a "bitterness of spirit," let alone "a permanently darkened future," or even *"the* future" unless qualified as the *near* future. A very interesting feature of the poem is its capability of being read superficially as well as fully, and if so read it retracts its temporal reach sharply to the events and animadversions of a single one out of innumerable evenings—it assumes a totally different mood.

So far, the poem's place in the "House of Life" has been ignored. The "human interest" spoken of can, of course, be the more plausibly proffered and accepted because of its place in that sequence. It follows close upon "Known in Vain" (XXX):

> So it happeneth
> When Work and Will awake too late, to gaze
> After their life sailed by, and hold their breath.
> Ah! who shall dare to search through what sad maze

> Thenceforth their incommunicable ways
> Follow the desultory feet of Death?

Sonnet XXXI is "The Landmark":

> Was *that* the landmark? What,—the foolish well
>   Whose wave, low down, I did not stoop to drink . . .
> But lo! the path is missed, I must go back,
>   And thirst to drink when next I reach the spring. . . .
> Yet though no light be left nor bird now sing
>   As here I turn, I'll thank God, hastening,
> That the same goal is still on the same track.

And Sonnet XXXII is "A Dark Day":

> The gloom that breaks upon me with these airs
>   Is like the drops which strike the traveller's brow
>   Who knows not, darkling, if they bring him now
> Fresh storm, or be old rain the covert bears.
> Ah! bodes this hour some harvest of new tares,
>   Or hath but memory of the day whose plough
>   Sowed hunger once,—the night at length when thou,
> O prayer found vain, didst fall out from my prayers? . . .

This succession manifestly builds up an effect which is continued in the emotional tinge to be found in "The Hill Summit," and a context which prepares us for the kind of explanation Doughty provides. That context materializes primarily, however, in the phrase "loitered in the vale too long" and points to regret for lost or missed opportunity as the central theme: the sonnet "Lost Days" (XL) follows not far after. This is in basic harmony with Doughty's account, and also, but only up to a point, with Bowra's. Nevertheless, to interpret a poem from its context in an acknowledged sequence is a different matter from reading it in the light of external biographical indications; and even when reading this poem in its sequence, we do not have the guidance of a very specific narrative link, nor (unlike the "Willowwood" group) have the poems a group-title. Ultimately, in the genetic explanation of the particular phenomenon, the poem, every one of the biographical possibilities will have to play its part, and the full account of its germination is likely to combine all the hypotheses mentioned, and more. The precise communication of the poem, however, will need no less to be separately ascertained when considered in its setting in the "House of Life," if questions are not to be begged or the poem's statement obstructed or obscured.

Croce protests that, if a sentiment "that has really been experienced" is incorporated in a poem, "it is as useless to seek any longer the reality of that sentiment, as it is vain to seek a drop of water poured into the ocean." Spingarn, in proclaiming the gospel of Croce in the United States, criticized Sainte-Beuve, the naturalist of souls, for his theory that "literature is the expression of personality," calling this "a misleading half-truth, if by personality is meant, not the artistic personality which unfolds itself in the work of art, but the complex of external traits which the artist exhibits in his practical life." The present limited argument does not go as far as these. Nor does it pivot on the view of T. S. Eliot when (perhaps influenced by Spingarn, and therefore by Croce) he insists that "the emotion of art is impersonal." I argue merely that a poem must not be read via the poet's biography, that, indeed, it *cannot* truly be so read; for even if the poet's communication should correspond precisely with the nearest known biographical moment, this could be recognized only when the poem had been defined by the independent act of criticism. It is a fact of our existence in time, multiple of level though it be, that the poem itself will constitute an irreducible particularity in the history of the poet, perhaps repeating known particularities of the biography, but perhaps, and very often, not; and that it will always be its own point in the succession. Criticism it is, not biography, that must establish the character of that point in mental space-time, determining what is conveyed, what kind of thing is expressed. Criticism contributes to biography, not vice versa.

It is not part of my purpose to discredit the natural, legitimate, and valuable interest in biography. Biography has been employed in the very argument here put forward—employed as in any attempt to understand a man and his work; and our attempts to fathom the relationship between a poet's poetry and his life are, furthermore, a part of our endeavor to understand the nature of poetry and thereby extend and justify our critical criteria. The Rossetti poem, for instance, set alongside the known biography, would seem to support the view that, where a poet in the act of composition is affected by *real, actual* emotionality, the reader will be invited to produce a simulated, spurious emotional response: that view has a number of obvious theoretic implications. Biography, moreover, as a possible source of clues to meaning, can only foolishly be ostracized by criticism; but in this respect it is merely a supplement to the dictionary—which will never do more than furnish the correct parts for the machine.

The case rests on "The Hill Summit" (and, without its context, *that* sentence might need the help of biography): a single instance is enough for establishing or rejecting the principle proposed. Any allegation that the biographical matter here juxtaposed with the poem has simply been inaccurate or insufficient confutes itself, as the effort to locate more and more finely the *right* piece of biography for a poem finds that the *exact* biographical moment is the poem itself, no more, no less, and no other. The "terrible" sonnets of Hopkins lie in an exceptionally detailed, large-scale biographical, indeed *auto*biographical documentation, far beyond what is available for Rossetti; but even they are none the more immune from misapprehension and consequent biographical misapplication from a "biographical" interpreting. The misjudging would be similar to that applied to Eliot's Prufrock by someone who knew of the St. Louis businessman who bore the name in Eliot's youth, and who felt compelled to limit the import of the result to that of its origin.

The indubitably autobiographical character of many novels will not exempt them from this law; and even *Jane Eyre* and *Villette, Evan Harrington, New Grub Street,* or Trilling's *Middle of the Journey,* or, as *Stephen Hero* shows, Joyce's *Portrait of the Artist,* must first submit to the uncovering fingers of criticism if they are to yield their true biographical message. They are no less susceptible than a sonnet is to discoloration by biography-tinted spectacles. The reverse process (or later stage), the extracting of biographical truth from the fictive history (or the poem), is not the matter under discussion, but it has its own dangers; and it is in this connection that the precepts of Croce or Eliot have their direct application.

Throughout this essay the validity, in principle, of biographical deduction from a work of literature has been accepted; there has been no affirming that the work of art stands free, totally and absolutely, of its maker and his history. And there will be no voicing of an *a fortiori*. The intention has been only to counsel biography to wait its turn, and to help fortify a position before the "human interest" forces arrive again, freshly armed with Hardy and his Tryphaena and bent on the suspension of critical rights. A palace of art need not be built to the plan of Tennyson's, nor furnished in the same fashion, and to invoke that particular lordly pleasure-house entails no commitment to an "aesthete's" system. It expresses only the belief that, whether a cottage in the vale or something grander or meaner, a house of life which comes on offer in the mode of art can only be opened up satisfactorily from within the art itself. Diamonds are carbon, but carbon is not diamonds; and whatever the organic relationship between the leaf, the blossom, and the bole, none of them is the roots, nor is the great-rooted blossomer the soil it grows in.

William Carlos Williams
and the Whitman Tradition
❖ ❖ ❖

JAMES E. BRESLIN

IN RECENT criticism of William Carlos Williams a major tendency has been to examine him ahistorically—as if he had been self-created.[1] Williams himself, an ardent egotist and violent antitraditionalist, often encouraged such an approach by denying or hiding his historical origins. At the same time, however, a constant return to sources was essential to the way in which Williams went about creating himself. He once complained of the "unstudied character of our beginnings" in America[2] and two of his major works, *In the American Grain* and *Paterson,* attempt to arrive at self-understanding by means of historical understanding. Certainly, to understand him fully we must see him, as he saw himself, as the heir and successor of Walt Whitman—as the modern poet who would complete the revolution in American poetry and sensibility that Whitman had begun.

Near the end of his career, in a key passage at the close of the fourth book of *Paterson,* Williams offers an important acknowledgment of his derivation from Whitman. There, after a debate

1. See, for example, Linda W. Wagner, *The Poems of William Carlos Williams* (Middletown, Conn., 1964), or J. Hillis Miller, *Poets of Reality* (Cambridge, 1966), pp. 285–359.

2. *In the American Grain* (Norfolk, Conn., 1933), p. 109.

in which one voice insists "the sea is not our home" while another contends that "you must come to it," a man swims in from the sea, naps on the beach, rises, puts on a pair of faded overalls and a shirt with its sleeves rolled up, picks some beach plums, turns, and heads inland. This solitary and carefree rough is headed, Williams tells us in his *Autobiography,* "toward Camden where Walt Whitman, much traduced, lived the latter years of his life and died." [3]

Williams was thus culminating his poetic development as he had begun it—by identifying himself with Walt Whitman. The fourth book of *Paterson* was published in 1951. But almost forty years earlier, in 1914, Williams had written "The Wanderer," the poem in which he announced the direction of his later development and acknowledged Whitman as his starting point. Before 1914 Williams presented the curiously divided figure of a practicing physician who was also an attenuated young aesthete. When he was not picking lice out of the hair of children or delivering babies in the slums of Rutherford, he was writing sonnets like this one:

The Uses of Poesy

I've fond anticipation of a day
O'erfilled with pure diversion presently,
For I must read a lady poesy
The while we glide by many a leafy bay,

Hid deep in rushes, where at random play
The glossy black-winged May-flies, or whence flee
Hush-throated nestlings in alarm,
Whom we have idly frighted with our boat's long sway.

3. *The Autobiography of William Carlos Williams* (New York, 1951), p. 392.

> For, lest o'ersaddened by such woes as spring
> To rural peace from our meek onward trend,
> What else more fit? We'll draw the light latch-string
>
> And close the door of sense; then satiate wend,
> On poesy's transforming giant wing,
> To worlds afar whose fruits all anguish mend.[4]

The constricted young man who composed this pathetic assay at suavity was not sixteen; he was twenty-six. We ought to remember, however, that revolutionaries, poetic or otherwise, are notoriously slow developers—Whitman himself is another example—and it may be, as Eric Erickson argues, that a prolonged period of constraint is necessary in order to generate and to articulate revolutionary energy.[5] In any event, when he wrote this sonnet, Williams, who later did write a poem about picking lice out of the hair of schoolchildren, clearly assumed a radical disjunction between poetry and his ordinary experience as a doctor and citizen in Rutherford. Closing the doors of the senses, this delicate young man, seated atop poesy's transforming giant wing, drifted into worlds remote, refined, and tranquil.

The story of Williams' early development is an account of a progression from this kind of aspiration for transcendence to an ardent desire to possess the immediate. As a young writer, Williams first thought he was Keats, later thought he was Pound, but then, through a 1913 reading of *Leaves of Grass,* discovered he was William Carlos Williams. The assertion of his own mature identity, along with an explicit rejection of his earlier aestheticism, comes in the final scene of "The Wanderer," where the young poet, anticipating the scene on the beach in

4. *Poems* (Rutherford, N. J., 1909), p. 11.
5. See Eric Erickson's *Young Man Luther* (New York, 1958).

Book IV of *Paterson,* leaps into "the Passaic, that filthy river." [6]
Repudiating an attitude of aloof refinement, he here disperses
himself into the contemporary world, which, in spite of its
degradation, he now identifies as the source of poetry:

> Then the river began to enter my heart,
> Eddying back cool and limpid
> Into the crystal beginning of its days.
> But with the rebound it leaped forward:
> Muddy, then black and shrunken
> Till I felt the utter depth of its rottenness
> The vile breadth of its degradation
> And dropped down knowing this was me now.

> *(CEP,* 11)

This immersion of the poet, like the one in the fourth book of
Paterson, enacts a re-creation of the self. Leaping into the con-
taminated river or the chaotic Atlantic, Williams annihilates his
identity and penetrates the physical world. But both scenes, while
they begin with a descent, end with the emergence of the poet,
renewed. The *Paterson* episode closes with the swimmer strolling
inland, affirming that the sea is not our home; and "The
Wanderer" ends not with the poet's surrender but with his
ascent, as he moves off on a "new wandering" *(CEP,* 12). In
each case, the movement is from a sympathetic dispersal into
otherness toward a reassertion of the self. This violent process of
renewal is at the center of Williams' poetry and, as he himself
recognized, its blending of an ardent sympathy with a bold
assertiveness directly connects him with Walt Whitman.

6. *The Collected Earlier Poems of William Carlos Williams* (Norfolk,
Conn., 1951), p. 11. Subsequent references will be made in the text to
CEP.

Among contemporary poets, Williams emerges as perhaps our most authentic heir of Whitman. At the same time, however, Williams *is* a modern, a member of a generation profoundly suspicious of untrammeled emotional release and the idealistic philosophy which encouraged it. For the moderns, the career of Whitman could have provided an apt illustration of the dilemma of romanticism. In America, transcendentalism, by affirming the metamorphic powers of the human mind, liberated the creative powers of the generation that included Whitman; but the trouble with heeding Emerson's injunction to "build therefore your own world," as Whitman soon discovered, was that you became its sole inhabitant. Only a few years after the first edition of *Leaves of Grass,* Whitman was no longer chanting joyfully of his sovereignty, his identification with the cosmos, but was now, withdrawn and melancholy, finding himself a solitary singer. Perhaps the principal task that T. S. Eliot accomplished for his generation was to objectify this problem in characters such as Tiresias, Gerontion, and J. Alfred Prufrock. In the early work of Eliot, all objects and values have been psychologized and the individual left in impenetrable isolation. "The Waste Land" internalizes the action of the traditional epic poem. "The Love Song of J. Alfred Prufrock" demonstrates that, if the perceiving mind transforms everything, then a man can connect himself with nothing.

Around 1913 a number of young writers, trying to break out of this constricting subjectivity, began connecting themselves with the object; the immediate poetic result was Imagism. In the critical polemics of this movement—mainly provided by Ezra Pound and T. E. Hulme—romantic work was dismissed as "fuzzy," "wet," "gummy," whereas good modern work was praised as "clean," "dry," "sharp-edged." In a deliberate reversal of the romantic tendency to dissolve the object by looking through it, these poets stressed the objective existence of the thing and the need to see it carefully and precisely. The modern artist characteristically insists that he is simply letting the objects speak for themselves—not transforming them to accord with his private moods. He is impersonal, self-effacing—more like a photographer than the dilating seer of romanticism.

To an important extent, Williams, with his characteristic precise, impersonal rendering of objects, was influenced by this movement. But the important thing to see is that his use of the object is shaped by his Whitmanian ardor and enthusiasm. The sharp, hard-edged quality of his work, its precise observation, is there to assure us that the emotion of the poem has been generated by *this* object—not brought to it by a rhapsodic poet. Williams' effacement before the object, like the leap into the sea or the river, is his way of becoming emotionally identified with it; self-abdication is part of the process of re-creation. His severely objective poems are thus essentially lyric—as a close look at his famous "The Red Wheelbarrow" will show:

> so much depends
> upon
>
> a red wheel
> barrow
>
> glazed with rain
> water
>
> beside the white
> chickens   (*CEP,* 277)

How can a poem about things as hopelessly and unutterably ordinary as a wheelbarrow and chickens be anything but flat? To a certain extent, Williams deliberately seeks banality and impersonality. The human element, the triumphant, celebrating "I" of Whitman's poetry, has disappeared; we get instead an impersonal assertion: "so much depends. . . ." With the disappearance of the poet comes an intense focus upon the object: short, jagged lines and long vowels slow down our movement through the poem, breaking off each part of the scene for careful observation. Any symbolic reading of the scene, a possible imposition by the observer, is carefully resisted; its hard, objective reality is insisted upon.

But Williams risks banality in order to push through to startling discoveries. The scene is not entirely bare: the wheelbarrow is red and it has just been rained on, giving its surface a fresh, "glazed" appearance. A spare, clinical manner, it is clear, asserts by relief the primary color and novelty that are there. Similarly, the effect of the impersonal subject, "so much," is not to empty the poem of emotion but to fill it with the ecstatic feeling which these particulars inspire. By its slow movement the poem not only forces us to concentrate upon the physical scene but also renders the intensity of the emotion; intensity means a stretching out. Originally, there is the feeling of a laborious push downward, away from all conscious forms of activity and toward a heightened receptivity; but the final effect is the sense of a slow lifting, with the uncovering of beauty in the ordinary. The poem *is* impersonal; but its impersonality is not that of the indifferent God, paring his fingernails, but one which comes from the way the poet has yielded himself intimately to the scene. The particulars in the poem, broken apart to be seen clearly, are drawn together by the ecstatic feeling generated by the poet's discovery. "The Red Wheelbarrow," far from being flat, convinces us we have spent our lives in a kind of blurred consciousness, a weary state that produces poems such as "The Uses of Poesy."

The brief, intense lyric poems—such as "The Red Wheelbarrow"—that fill the pages of Williams' collected works are the product of his desire for a constant renewal of the self. The theory of mind behind this impetus is worth making explicit. According to Williams, mental activity in most people is conducted primarily at the level of the ordinary consciousness or the ego. The distinctive feature of such life is its tendency toward a rigid conservatism, a fear of new experience, and a desire to operate safely and fixedly within established categories. Locked within a system, cut off from fresh experience by the desire for security, the ordinary man will be emotionally and sensually starved; in a real sense, he will not even exist. "The reader," Williams writes in the prose commentary in *Spring and All,*

knows himself as he was twenty years ago and he has also in mind a vision of what he would be, some day. Oh, some day! But the thing he never knows and never dares to know is what he is at the exact moment that he is. And this moment is the only thing in which I am at all interested.[7]

Ironically, then, the person who seeks security uproots himself from the present moment, the only thing that *is,* and so he becomes a perpetual drifter. Because he is impoverished, his activity will be incessant; but because he is dissociated from the sources of life, his restless activity will be futile. The ordinary American,

7. *Spring and All* (Dijon, 1923), pp. 2–3.

in Williams' view, is a man whose swift-moving commitment to material ends has abstracted him from immediate experience—from the New World; his fear of the new, thwarting the creative process of renewal, is self-destructive.

Yet the restless dissatisfaction which drives such a man to act is the expression of a deeper level of personality, a buried self, a rebellious force that Williams identifies with our physical being. If we release this primal power, we hear, Williams believed, "the deeper, not the lower (in the usually silly sense) portions of the personality speaking, the middle brain, the nerves, the glands, the very muscles and bones of the body itself speaking." [8] By means of this primitive level of personality we can break out of the locked world of the ego and renew our participation in "the rhythmic ebb and flow of the mysterious life process." [9] The release of the buried self is thus equivalent to the leap into the Passaic at the end of "The Wanderer," an act which immerses the poet in the fluid process of life. The kind of objective lyric he writes, in which the poet melts into the scene, is thus Williams' artistic way of perpetually renewing himself.

This process is also the source of Whitman's poetry. While we usually think of Whitman as arrogantly chanting "the chant of dilation or pride," he constantly expands himself by disappearing into a scene—an event that occurs in the famous fifth section of "Song of Myself."

Swiftly arose and spread around me the peace and knowledge that
    pass all the argument of the earth,

8. "How to Write," *New Directions in Prose and Poetry*, No. 1 (Norfolk, Conn., 1936), n.p.
    9. *Ibid.*

And I know that the hand of God is the promise of my own,
And I know that the spirit of God is the brother of my own,
And that all the men ever born are also my brothers, and the women
my sisters and lovers,
And that a kelson of the creation is love,
And limitless are leaves stiff or drooping in the fields,
And brown ants in the little wells beneath them,
And mossy scabs of the worm fence, heap'd stones, elder, mullein
and poke-weed.

The passage beautifully evokes Whitman's special state of conscious ecstasy—a transport in which the senses remain awake. At first, he dilates with the certain knowledge of his divine power, but gradually the insistent "I know" and even the "that" are dropped as the poet literally scatters himself through the entire creation. Whitman disappears because he is everywhere: he is God, he is poke-weed, he is love, binding together the universe. The cosmic scale in Whitman is obviously much larger than in Williams, who needs to concentrate his powers before he can release them; but the dispersal into the world serves the same end in both poets.

"The Red Wheelbarrow" first appeared in *Spring and All* (1923), the most impressive volume of verse that Williams ever produced. In that volume, the culmination of a decade of fitful, rather dispersive experiment, Williams' achievement was more sustained and more various than it ever was to be again. The sense of a steady accomplishment in *Spring and All* is all the more remarkable because that volume appeared just after one of the most unsettling events of Williams' career—the publication of "The Waste Land." "I shall never forget the impression created by *The Waste Land,*" Williams writes in "An Essay on *"Leaves of Grass."* "It was as if the bottom had dropped out of everything. I had not known how much the spirit of Whitman animated us until it was withdrawn from us."[10] The vigorous spirit of Whitman had indeed been withdrawn from the dominant line of American poetry, not to reappear until the middle of the 1950s. But, as Williams himself implies, the impact of Eliot's poem helped Williams to identify himself at the same time that it threatened and frustrated him. Williams now had a role, messianic in its ambitions, to play in American poetry and American culture. In Whitman, Williams had a revolutionary predecessor whose acceptance of the new world he hoped to generate among his contemporaries and in Eliot he had a feudal contemporary who provided an exact focus for all his poetic and social repudiations. Williams himself emerges as the beleaguered prophet of revolutionary energy, democratic acceptance, and Whitmanian ardor.

By contradicting Whitman's myth of plenitude with the myth of sterility, Eliot prompted Williams to identify his own informing myth—the discovery of plenty lodged, as it must be in the modern world, in barrenness. In the first few years of the twenties Williams' work grew out of his own experience of postwar disillusionment. "Damn it," he writes in the *Autobiography,*

the freshness, the newness of a springtime which I had sensed among the others, a reawakening of letters, all that delight which in making

10. In *Whitman: A Collection of Essays,* ed. Roy H. Pearce (Englewood Cliffs, N.J., 1962), p. 148.

a world to match the supremacies of the past could mean was being blotted out by the war. The stupidity, the calculated viciousness of a money-grubbing society such as I knew and violently wrote against; everything I wanted to see live and thrive was being deliberately murdered in the name of church and state.[11]

The feeling in Williams' work of the period is not quite one of despair, but of life buried, maintaining itself underground, in a kind of hell, but powerless to assert itself. In *Sour Grapes* (1921), Williams constantly gives us images of life buried but persisting in winter or old age. The year before, he had found the mythological counterpart to his situation in the story of Kora or Persephone. Kora, while gathering wildflowers on Mount Enna, was abducted by Pluto and taken to the underworld. With her disappearance the earth became barren. Eventually, Demeter, her mother, succeeded in freeing her—but only for nine months of the year; the other three she had to spend in the underworld. Kora is thus a fertility goddess whose yearly round signifies the burial of the seed and the return of vegetation. In 1920 Williams wrote a book of prose improvisations, *Kora in Hell*, the blighting of the creative principle: "Kora," he says, "was the springtime of the year; my year, my self was being slaughtered." [12] In *Spring and All* Williams shifts his attention to the moment of generation, the reassertion of the life buried in winter. The title of the volume is significant; with the return of spring, a Whitmanian acceptance of all once again becomes possible.

Characteristic of the poems in this volume, "The Eyeglasses" begins with descriptions of the flowers that grow near the edges

11. *Autobiography,* p. 158.   12. *Ibid.*

of refuse heaps and of the delicate beauty of the daughter issuing from the gross strength of the farmer:

> The universality of things
> draws me toward the candy
> with melon flowers that open
>
> about the edge of refuse
> proclaiming without accent
> the quality of the farmer's
>
> shoulders and his daughter's
> accidental skin, so sweet
> with clover and the small
>
> yellow cinquefoil in the
> parched places.   (*CEP*, 256)

The constant subject of the poems in *Spring and All* is the emergence of life out of death, ecstasy out of despair, poetry unexpectedly blossoming in a parched industrial landscape. The shift in the outer world, as Williams' identification with the spring suggests, corresponds to an inner change—and so the real subject of these poems is the re-creation of the self.

Like so many works of the twenties, the book is apocalyptic in tone; a prose commentary, which opens the volume and accompanies the poems throughout, begins with a vision of cataclysmic destruction. Yet the approaching crisis excites Williams. The root sense of apocalypse is "uncover" and what excites Williams is the possibility that the upheaval will uncover Persephone, the buried creative principle. The self which J. Alfred Prufrock covers with the face he prepares to meet the faces that he meets can be released, Williams believed, "by a mere twist of the imagination." [13] "It is spring," he says after the catastrophe in *Spring and All,* "THE WORLD IS NEW." [14] The major impetus behind this book is an affirmation of a creative force which is often hidden, surrounded by blankness, but which ardent pursuit can still uncover.

The four books of poetry Williams had written since "The Wanderer" all began with a spring poem. But in 1923, as the poet of birth in a seemingly sterile environment, Williams imagined a new spring for poetry: he became the poet of March, the beginning of the beginning. The awakening of creativity, captured very precisely, provides the subject for the first poem in *Spring and All,* the austerely beautiful "By the road to the contagious hospital."

> By the road to the contagious hospital
> under the surge of the blue
> mottled clouds driven from the
> northeast—a cold wind. Beyond, the
> waste of broad, muddy fields
> brown with dried weeds, standing and fallen
>
> patches of standing water
> the scattering of tall trees
>
> All along the road the reddish
> purplish, forked, upstanding, twiggy
> stuff of bushes and small trees
> with dead, brown leaves under them
> leafless vines—

13. *Selected Essays of William Carlos Williams* (New York, 1954), p. 22.

14. *Spring and All,* pp. 10–11.

> Lifeless in appearance, sluggish
> dazed spring approaches—
>
> They enter the new world naked,
> cold, uncertain of all
> save that they enter. All about them
> the cold, familiar wind—
>
> Now the grass, tomorrow
> the stiff curl of wildcarrot leaf
> One by one objects are defined—
> It quickens: clarity, outline of leaf
>
> But now the stark dignity of
> entrance—Still, the profound change
> has come upon them: rooted, they
> grip down and begin to awaken   (*CEP,* 241–42)

This poem does not simply render the physical qualities of the landscape; its center is an action, "the stark dignity of/ entrance," the slow penetration of the landscape by an awakening observer. We follow the thrust of the imagination downward, through obstacles, to new union with the physical environment. The progression in the poem is literally downward: the poet moves from "the blue/ mottled clouds," across a distant view of "broad, muddy fields," to the quickening plant life right before him— and then penetrates even further down as he imagines the roots taking hold in the earth. The panoramic view, with its prospect of "muddy fields," "dried weeds," "patches of standing water," offers nothing with which the imagination might joyously connect itself. At first, an apparently blank and "lifeless" nature invites the observer to passivity and despair; but Williams, once again, pushes through blankness to uncover novelty.

Implicitly "By the road" argues that Eliot's despair derives from his cosmopolitanism, his detachment from a locality. What the tenacious observer here finally perceives is not a "waste" land but a "new world" and he makes his discovery by narrowing and focusing Whitman's panoramic vision upon the low and the ordinary. In the torpor of ordinary consciousness what we find "by the road to the contagious hospital" is a desolate landscape. But the awakened mind, focused sharply, can discover novelty and life, the first "sluggish/ dazed" stirrings of spring. Hence, poet and landscape are gradually identified—as he too grips down and begins to awaken.

In Eliot's early poetry, always spoken by "voices dying with a dying fall," the characteristic movement is the fall of anticlimax —as, for instance, Prufrock's aspirations for communion are thwarted by his fears of self-exposure. In Williams, movement is typically through a slow, downward thrust toward an ecstatic lift—or through a backward push toward a liberating assertion forward. His poems attempt to renew us by taking us down to the physical world, back to our origins, in order to generate creative force. In "By the road," even after he has discovered the burgeoning life in the amorphous "stuff" around him, Williams slips forward into a dream of April definition: "tomorrow/ the stiff curl of wildcarrot leaf." The abrupt shift back to a concentration upon the "now" in the final stanza partly accounts for its force. Again, Williams' subject is the not triumphant rising of new life in April, but the very origins of life in an atmosphere of death, desolation, and contagion.

These rough, jerky down-up, back-forward movements are the structural sources of the sense of brokenness that Williams' verse gives. This disjunctiveness, in turn, helps to convince the reader that the movement in the poem is genuinely free—that it is not a mechanical progression toward a predetermined end. At the same time, the roughness of the poem supplies the radical jolt necessary to jar the reader out of ordinary consciousness. Sometimes, the result is a kind of surrealistic poem, in which the images are not derived from any "real" physical scene but seem to float brokenly in space. This kind of poem, still impersonal in tone, precise in its imagery, is a variant of the objective lyric that Williams customarily writes—and it shows the flexibility of that form. Among the *Spring and All* poems, a violent distortion of normal reality appears in "At the Faucet of June," "Young Love," "The Eyeglasses," and "The Agonized Spires." The lines quoted earlier from "The Eyeglasses," for example, do not grow out of the poet's observation of a particular place: the melon flowers that grow by refuse heaps are linked with the farmer's daughter by an imaginative, not a physical, proximity. As two instances of beauty emerging from grossness, they belong together in an imaginative category. This poem, in which Williams speaks of "the favorable/distortion of eyeglasses," contains the justification of its own method: actualities are distorted in order to be seen more accurately and intensely.

The first stanza of "St. Francis Einstein of the Daffodils," a poem not in *Spring and All* but first written in 1921, provides an even better example of this surrealistic mode:

> "Sweet land"
> at last!
> out of the sea—
> the Venus remembering wavelets

rippling with laughter—
freedom
for the daffodils!
—in a tearing wind
that shakes
the tufted orchards—
Einstein, tall as a violet
in the lattice-arbor corner
is tall as
a blossomy peartree   (*CEP,* 379)

In "At the Faucet of June" Williams conceives of the financier as
a modern Pluto whose rape of Persephone, the life principle,
generates the motor car, frightening image of approaching
catastrophe. The rape of the landscape by the industrialist is the
very opposite of the intimate union between man and the physical environment that Williams wants to bring about. In his
mythology, the hero is not the conquering capitalist but the self-
effacing man of science; not the person who appropriates energy
but the one who—like Madame Curie or Einstein—in a sense
releases it. The triumph of scientific discovery, unlike free enter-
prise, is not personal; and yet the scientist is a revolutionary creating a new world. Appropriately, then, Einstein the man disappears in this poem and is identified with the wind, the violet,
the peartree—with the creative principle itself. Instead of ravish-
ing Persephone, he merges with her. The disjunctiveness of the
series of phrases in the first stanza stresses the generative force of
his discovery—which breaks apart the ordinary world; and it also
helps to create the sense of freedom and gaiety inspired by the
occasion.

So far, we have been looking at Williams as a poet of acceptance and discovery; but many of his poems reveal the frightening consequences of the desire to escape from the arduous pursuit of the new. The banality of the here and now is such that the desire for escape will exercise a strong and frequent pull. But the continual threat to identity is that a man, abandoning the physical which is the source of life, will drift off in fantasies of quick, easy self-fulfillment. Such dreams, their hypnotic appeal but final horror, initiate the action of a number of poems. "The Yachts" (*CEP,* 106–7), in which the consequences of the desire for swift, graceful, unimpeded movement are devastatingly revealed, provides the most impressive instance of this technique. Among the *Spring and All* poems, "The Sea" (*CEP,* 275–76) deals with the desire to escape from the tensions of individual life by a simple surrender to the forces of nature.

> The sea that encloses her young body
> ula lu la lu
> is the sea of many arms—
>
> The blazing secrecy of noon is undone
> and and and
> the broken sand is the sound of love—

This poem *begins* by lifting us out of ordinary reality: we do not hear the rough, harsh music of "By the road" but the full, euphonious song of a mermaid inviting us to drift, easily, into transcendence. With its smooth, incantatory music, this poem—like the sea—urges us to yield to it—an urge, however, which we finally reject. The way the poet is playfully euphonious, mockingly incantatory, keeps us from submitting to the hypnotic spell—as does his awakened sense of "the sea that is cold with dead men's tears." The pull here is not toward the active, sympathetic possession of the natural but toward a passive surrender to it. The result of such a yielding, the end of the poem makes plain, is a dispersal of the self into nothingness:

> Underneath the sea where it is dark
> there is no edge
> so two—

A few years before this poem was written, J. Alfred Prufrock had wandered along the beach and murmured of the mermaids, "I do not think that they will sing to me." The ruminating figure in Williams' poem, no man of attenuated intellect, is sensual enough to hear the song of the mermaids and resilient enough to resist it. This poem affirms, once again, that a tension between man and his environment is the source of his identity.

For a poet residing in Rutherford, New Jersey, especially a poet with prophetic ambitions, the pull toward the great city across the river must have been a persistent one. The third poem in *Spring and All* is "The Farmer"—in which Williams presents "the artist figure of/the farmer" as one who contends with and eventually triumphs over the "blank fields" of March. The next poem, "Flight to the City" (*CEP*, 244), evolves out of the yearning for a quick ascent in the great city. Here the pull is upward, away from the physical. While the farmer looks down at "browned weeds," the speaker in "Flight" gazes at the stars, traditional emblems of lofty aspiration, and muses in a lyric style expressive of his desire to lift himself out of the desolate climate of Rutherford.

                    The Easter stars are shining
                    above lights that are flashing—
                    coronal of the black—

But a flat, prosaic voice abruptly interrupts this wistful lyricism:

                            Nobody
            to say it—
                    Nobody to say: pinholes

These two voices initiate a characteristic back-and-forth move‑
ment toward a view of the city as a place of false and impoverish‑
ing dreams.

                    Thither I would carry her

                    among the lights—

                    Burst it asunder
                    break through to the fifty words
                    necessary—

                            a crown for her head with
                    castles on it, skyscrapers
                    filled with nut-chocolates—

                                    dovetame winds—
                    stars of tinsel

                    from the great end of a cornucopia
                    of glass

As in "The Sea," the playfulness—here in the fairy tale quality of
the imagery—distances the reader from the dream and helps to
prepare him for the final reversal. As always in Williams, the
process is a slow stripping away of conventional associations—

here toward a revelation of a city whose plenty cannot nourish.

With supreme confidence, the Whitman of 1855 could saunter down the streets of New York City, wander along the shores of the Atlantic, disperse himself into the crowd or the sea and yet retain his simple, separate identity. The desire to merge with the surging life of the great city or the ocean is frequent in Williams; these are tensions organic to his locality, in Rutherford, but they must be resisted. In Williams, images of totality are always images of an unformed mass which threatens to crush the individual. That is why both the Atlantic and New York become images of nothingness, voids in which the individual will disintegrate. And that is why he writes in "The Wildflower" that "crowds are white"; Whitman's *en-masse* has become destructive. The difference is that for Williams the physical world, initially at least, is neutral: "They enter the new world naked,/ cold, uncertain of all/ save that they enter." The imagination can only possess fragments. As he writes in "To Elsie,"

> It is only in isolate flecks that
> something
> is given off   (*CEP,* 272)

For Williams, the sea is not our home; his sources are in the hard, definite earth, the limited compass of a small town. He is not advocating flight from the pull of these vast forces; he is simply urging movement into a defined area in which chaos can be contended with successfully. His scope is not as vast as Whitman's; but he seeks a similar organic extension of the self.

"Why do you write?" Williams asked himself in a dialogue-essay. "For relaxation, relief," he replied. "To have nothing in my head—to freshen my eye by that till I see, smell, know and can reason and be."[15] By a curious circular process, creative activity, which begins by subverting rational processes, ends by initiating them. Much more often than his critics have noticed, Williams works as a reflective poet. It is true that Williams was not a man of subtle, fertile, or even systematic intellect. But he did have a ruminative quality of mind—a quality frequently found in the verse, which often describes the mind as it gropes toward a moment of apprehension. "The goal," he writes, "is to keep a beleaguered line of understanding which has movement from breaking down and becoming a hole into which we sink decoratively to rest."[16] Since the line of advance, as always in Williams, is beleaguered, these reflective poems are radically disjunctive. Williams is so eager to avoid what he calls the "managed poem," which imposes an ideology on experience, that his meditative works become broken to an extent that often makes them difficult to penetrate.[17] But at his best he creates the impression of an incisive and passionate mind in the *act* of generating thought. The reflective poems, like those which grow more directly out of observation, move us slowly but compactly toward a jolting discovery.

"The rose is obsolete," Williams muses at the beginning of "The Rose" (*CEP,* 249–50), but an act of the imagination can make even this traditional symbol new. In this poem, one of the

15. *Selected Essays,* p. 101.   16. *Ibid.,* p. 118.
17. "An Approach to the Poem," in *English Institute Essays* (New York, 1948), p. 59.

many reflective works in *Spring and All,* Williams proceeds from a consideration of the way to renew the impact of the flower to a joyous affirmation of its rediscovered power. "The Rose" appears at a point in the prose commentary of *Spring and All* at which Williams praises the Cubist painter Juan Gris for dealing with "things with which [the onlooker] is familiar, simple things—at the same time [detaching] them from ordinary experience to the imagination." [18] Williams thus takes the familiar rose and lifts it out of amorphous, ordinary contexts: he makes it inorganic by thinking of it as precisely cut onto "metal or porcelain" and abstracts even further by imagining it in a world of infinite, empty space. There, he contemplates it playfully, constantly turning his argument on the ambiguity of the word "end." "The rose carried weight of love," he says, "but love is at an end—of roses." Just as he constantly asserts that life must be caught as it emerges out of death, so here he argues that at the end of the rose, its death and its edge, a new beginning can be found.

To see the rose anew, he argues, we must concentrate upon the locus of its singularity—its edges. Raised from a flat surface, carefully worked onto china, these edges can be seen distinctly.

> Sharper, neater, more cutting
> figured in majolica—
> the broken plate
> glazed with a rose

Only when the flower has been worked painstakingly onto a hard, inorganic substance will its fragile life be preserved—a paradox which subtly informs his meditation.

18. *Spring and All,* p. 34.

                    Crisp, worked to defeat
                    laboredness—fragile
                    plucked, moist, half-raised
                    cold, precise, touching

In its abstracted realm, however, the rose touches—nothing; there
is a surrounding blankness which at once threatens and defines
the flower. When he speaks of need to have objects or words
with "hard edges," Williams is using a phrase found in the
writings of a whole gamut of moderns—from Hemingway to
Wittgenstein. But to Williams the importance of the edge is that
it is, as here in "The Rose," the place of maximum tension and
thus of maximum life; that is why Williams likes to think of
himself in his prose writings as a man on the margin. But the
important point is that clear perception, seeing the hard-edged
particularity of the object, generates a force or an emotion—as
Williams affirms in the closing lines of "The Rose":

                    From the petal's edge a line starts
                    that being of steel
                    infinitely fine, infinitely
                    rigid penetrates
                    the Milky Way
                    without contact—lifting
                    from it—neither hanging
                    nor pushing—

                    The fragility of the flower
                    unbruised
                    penetrates space.

The image is a bold and striking one, but nevertheless characteristic: a delicate life, a fine line—emerging out of the dead

porcelain—triumphantly asserts its distinction through infinite space.

The need for assertion as well as surrender is thus central in these poems. To Williams, surrender, the attitude in which Whitman carelessly leaned and loafed and invited his soul, is a position in which the self is precariously exposed. Williams' imagination—not too surprisingly—is more masculine than Whitman's: Whitman's world is so abundant, so perfectly harmonious, that he can simply relax and wait to be ravished by it—but Williams, whose world is splintered, neutral, must seek more actively to possess it. Lying down, Williams reminds us, is the attitude of humiliation—"like a patient etherized upon a table" —as well as the position in which we make love. In *Spring and All* Williams thus remarks: "The inevitable flux of the seeing eye toward measuring itself by the world it inhabits can only result in . . . crushing humiliation unless the individual raise to some approximate coextension with the universe."[19] Being swept along by the flux annihilates the personality yet at the same time stirs a compensating desire for untrammeled freedom and quick mastery. But the desire for such ascendency, as we know from "Flight to the City," severs the individual from the physical and so ironically culminates in real loss of self. Williams' famous poem "The Yachts" illustrates this process; the swift, free grace of the boats can be attained only in a "well-guarded arena" which shields them from "the too heavy blows/ of an ungoverned ocean." Gradually, the reductive quality of the scene is transferred to the men on the yachts who, apparently masterful, be-

19. *Ibid.,* pp. 26–27.

come "ant-like" and, in the final lines of the poem, disappear as the "skillful yachts"—not skillful men—drive over suffering, impotent humanity. The terrifying impact of this poem comes not just from Williams' transformation of a conventional symbol of freedom into one of brutality but also from the impersonality of the instruments of oppression as they are driven along, uncontrolled, by the rushing wind. This is the very reverse of the sympathetic self-effacement that Williams seeks.

In "To Elsie" (*CEP,* 270–71) Williams contemplates the terrifying consequences of surrendering to the dominant American mythology. Here, Williams generates out of the lower-class world of his locality what he saw in the upper-class world in "The Yachts"—a nightmare vision of America, the sense of approaching apocalypse. A pure product of America, one of the famous Jackson Whites of northern New Jersey, Williams' hulking, half-mad maid, Elsie, expresses with her "broken/ brain the truth about us." Addressing herself "to cheap/ jewelry/ and rich young men with fine eyes," she embodies the national desire for quick, gaudy wealth. The myth of success, with which Williams, the child of immigrants, was imbued in his youth, became part of his mature demonology. For what Elsie signifies is a culture in which aspirations are not fed by an organic relation to the physical environment. In their deepest selves, Williams argues, most Americans, like the original settlers of this continent, believe that this world is a dunghill. We act, he writes,

> as if the earth under our feet
> were
> an excrement of some sky

     and we degraded prisoners
     destined
     to hunger until we eat filth

     while the imagination strains
     after deer
     going by fields of goldenrod in

     the stifling heat of September

Our dreams of heavenly tranquillity, of a paradise above, disso-
ciate us from the real sources of life right under our bootsoles. At
the end of the poem Williams fixes a culture whose products are
locked, impenetrable, swift-moving, and brutal in the image of a
driverless car.

     No one
     to witness
     and adjust, no one to drive the car

  The unmanned yachts and the driverless car: both are frightening images of a rapid, uncontrollable force—modern versions of
the myth of Pluto, god of avarice and rape. For individual
sustenance and social harmony, a controlling center is needed, a
place to stand in the surrounding flux, a center from which the
self goes out and to which it returns. Nothing could be further
from the truth than to argue, as J. Hillis Miller has done, that in
the final scene of "The Wanderer" Williams, once and for all,
annihilated his ego and became a humble, selfless, tranquil,
passionless poet of reality.[20] In the Preface to his *Autobiography*
Williams calls the sexual urge "the drive which empowers us
all"; but he quickly adds that "a man does with it what his mind

  20. *Poets of Reality,* p. 287.

directs." [21] The buried self is morally neutral: it can be creative or destructive, or both—depending upon the direction supplied by the ego. What Williams seeks is not abnegation of the ego but, like Whitman, a process by which the ego is constantly renewed. To bear witness is to give personal testimony; to say, in Whitman's words, "I was the man, I suffer'd, I was there." Williams' poems testify to the ardor and intimacy of his contact with the physical world—and do so in order to establish us in the surrounding flux; like Whitman's, his poems witness and adjust.

21. *Autobiography,* p. xi.

Supervising Committee
❖ ❖ ❖
The English Institute, 1966

The Program
❖ ❖ ❖
September 6 through September 9,
1966

CONFERENCES

I. *Troilus and Criseyde*
   Directed by Morton Bloomfield, Harvard University

   1. *Troilus and Criseyde:* The Art of Amplification
      Robert W. Frank, Jr., Pennsylvania State University

   2. Chaucer's Conception of Character in *Troilus and Criseyde*
      Charles Blyth, Columbia University

   3. Friendship in Chaucer's *Troilus*
      Alan T. Gaylord, University of Michigan

II. *Criticism and Biography*
   Directed by Irvin Ehrenpreis, University of Virginia

   1. Roles of the Victorian Critic
      Edward Alexander, University of Washington

   2. Autobiography and Art: An Elizabethan Hybrid
      Rudolf Gottfried, Indiana University

   3. Frost: The Biographer as Critic
      Lawrance Thompson, Princeton University

III. *William Carlos Williams*
   Directed by Reed Whittemore, Carleton College

   1. William Carlos Williams, 1883–1963: The Doctor's Poet
      William B. Ober, M.D., New York Medical College

2. William Carlos Williams: The Bridge at the Boundary
   Muriel Rukeyser, Sarah Lawrence College

3. William Carlos Williams: The Fecund Minimum
   Mark Linenthal, San Francisco State College

IV. *Criticism and History*
   Directed by Larzer Ziff, University of California, Berkeley

   1. Sophocles, Freud, and the Timeless World of Criticism
      Simon Lesser, University of Massachusetts

   2. History and Idea in Renaissance Criticism
      Phillip Damon, University of California, Berkeley

   3. The Abuses of History in the Criticism of Fiction
      Wayne Booth, University of Chicago

PRIZE ESSAYS

"Two Boethian Speeches and Chaucerian Irony in *Troilus and Criseyde*"
   Peter Elbow, Brandeis University
"The Study of Literature and the Recovery of the Historical"
   Warner Berthoff, Bryn Mawr College

Honorable Mention

"The Lay of Paterson"
   A. D. Van Nostrand, Brown University
"Whitman and the Early Development of William Carlos Williams"
   James E. Breslin, University of California, Berkeley

Registrants

❖ ❖ ❖

1966

Hazard Adams, University of California, Irvine; Ruth Adams, Wellesley College; Edward Alexander, University of Washington; Gellert S. Alleman, Rutgers University, Newark; George P. Allen, Oxford University Press; Marcia Allentuck, City College, New York; Hugh Amory, Columbia University; Reta Anderson, Emory University; Valborg Anderson, Brooklyn College; Mother Mary Anthony, Rosemont College; Richard W. Arthur, Rutgers University; George W. Bahlke, Middlebury College; Ashur Baizer, Ithaca College; Sheridan Baker, University of Michigan; Stewart A. Baker, Rice University; Frank Baldanza, Bowling Green State University; C. L. Barber, Indiana University; Mrs. E. F. Barber, Duke University; Richard Barksdale, Atlanta University; Lynn C. Bartlett, Vassar College; L. A. Beaurline, University of Virginia; Rev. John E. Becker, s.j., Yale University; John Benedict, W. W. Norton & Co.; Warner B. Berthoff, Bryn Mawr College; Siegmund A. E. Betz, Our Lady of Cincinnati College; Rev. Vincent F. Blehl, s.j., Fordham University; Mother M. Blish, Manhattanville College of the Sacred Heart; Morton W. Bloomfield, Harvard University; Charles R. Blyth, Jr., Columbia University; Wayne C. Booth, University of Chicago; Rev. John D. Boyd, s.j., Fordham University; James E. Breslin, University of California, Berkeley; Henry L. Brooks, North Carolina College; Richard A. E. Brooks, Vassar College; Rev. George Hardin Brown, s.j., Harvard University; Margaret M. Bryant, Brooklyn College; Jean R. Buchert, University of North Carolina, Greensboro; Janet T. Buck, Douglass College; Charles O. Burgess, Old Dominion College; Brother Fidelian Burke, f.s.c., La Salle College; Sister M. Vincentia Burns, Albertus Magnus College; George E. Bush, St.

Francis College; Mervin Butovsky, Sir George Williams University; Robert Buttel, Temple University; Kathleen Byrne, Ligonier, Pennsylvania; Grace J. Calder, Hunter College; John A. Cameron, Amherst College; Ronald Campbell, Harcourt, Brace & World, Inc.; G. H. Carrithers, Jr., State University of New York, Buffalo; B. A. Casey, University of Rochester; Sister Mary Charles, I.H.M., Immaculata College; Hugh C. G. Chase, Milton, Massachusetts; Howell D. Chickering, Jr., Amherst College; Kent Christensen, Upsala College; Mother Mary Clement, S.H.C.J., School of the Holy Child; James L. Clifford, Columbia University; Robert A. Colby, Queens College; Arthur N. Collins, State University of New York, Albany; Rowland L. Collins, Indiana University; Ralph W. Condee, Pennsylvania State University; John Conley, Queens College; Thomas W. Copeland, University of Massachusetts; G. Armour Craig, Amherst College; Robert P. Creed, State University of New York, Stony Brook; Lucille Crighton, Gulf Park College; J. V. Cunningham, Brandeis University; R. Cunningham, R.S.C.J., Manhattanville College of the Sacred Heart; Rev. John V. Curry, S.J., Loyola Seminary; Charles R. Dahlberg, Queens College; Phillip Damon, University of California, Berkeley; Lloyd J. Davidson, Virginia Military Institute; Winifred M. Davis, Hunter College; Robert Adams Day, Queens College; Charlotte D'Evelyn, Mt. Holyoke College; E. T. Donaldson, Yale University; John H. Dorenkamp, Holy Cross College; George Dorris, Queens College; Victor Doyno, Princeton University; Edgar H. Duncan, Vanderbilt University; Ivar L. M. Duncan, Belmont College; Thomas F. Dunn, Canisius College; David A. Dushkin, Random House, Inc.; Edward R. Easton, Pace College; Thomas R. Edwards, Jr., Rutgers University; Irvin Ehrenpreis, University of Virginia; Peter Elbow, Brandeis University; Mother Mary Eleanor, S.H.C.J., Rosemont College; Sister Elizabeth Marian, College of Mt. St. Vincent; Scott Elledge, Cornell University; Robert C. Elliott, University of California, San Diego; Richard Ellmann, Northwestern University; Martha W. England, Queens College; David V. Erdman, New York Public Library; Sister Marie Eugénie, I.H.M., Immaculata College; H. Alfred Farrell, Lincoln University; Sylvia D.

Feldman, Emory University; Arthur Fenner, Jr., University of Detroit; Edward G. Fletcher, University of Texas; Ephim G. Fogel, Cornell University; French Fogle, Claremont Graduate School; Robert Folkenflik, Cornell University; George H. Ford, University of Rochester; Robert D. Foulke, Trinity College; Richard Lee Francis, Brown University; Robert W. Frank, Jr., Pennsylvania State University; Albert B. Friedman, Claremont Graduate School; Edwin Fussell, Claremont Graduate School; Paul Fussell, Jr., Rutgers University; Harry R. Garvin, Bucknell University; Alan T. Gaylord, University of Michigan; Anthony Gosse, Bucknell University; Sister Mary Eugene Gotimer, College of Mt. St. Vincent; Rudolf B. Gottfried, Indiana University; Rev. Thomas Grace, s.j., Holy Cross College; John E. Grant, University of Iowa; James J. Greene, College of New Rochelle; Richard L. Greene, Wesleyan University; M. E. Grenander, State University of New York, Albany; Allen Guttmann, Amherst College; Victor M. Hamm, Marquette University; Sister Sara William Hanley, c.s.j., The College of St. Rose; Reginald L. Hannaford, Bowdoin College; Robert W. Hanning, Columbia College; John Edward Hardy, University of South Alabama; Richard Harrier, Washington Square College, New York University; John A. Hart, Carnegie Institute of Technology; Joan E. Hartman, Cambridge, Massachusetts; Harriett Hawkins, Vassar College; Ann L. Hayes, Carnegie Institute of Technology; Allen T. Hazen, Columbia University; Miriam M. Heffernan, Brooklyn College; John H. Hicks, University of Massachusetts; A. Kent Hieatt, Columbia College; Elizabeth K. Hill, Queens College; James L. Hill, Michigan State University; Rev. William Bernard Hill, s.j., Novitiate of St. Isaac Jogues; Laurence B. Holland, Princeton University; Frank S. Hook, Lehigh University; Vivian C. Hopkins, State University of New York, Albany; Muriel T. Hughes, University of Vermont; J. Paul Hunter, Emory University; Samuel Hynes, Swarthmore College; Julia T. Hysham, Skidmore College; W. R. Irwin, University of Iowa; Sears Jayne, Queens College; W. T. Jewkes, Pennsylvania State University; S. F. Johnson, Columbia University; Leah E. Jordan, West Chester State College; R. M. Jordan, State University of New

York, Stony Brook; Stanley J. Kahrl, University of Rochester; John
E. Keating, Kent State University; Robert Kellogg, University of
Virginia; Norman Kelvin, City College of New York; Sister Eileen
Campion Kennedy, College of St. Elizabeth; James G. Kennedy,
Upsala College; Joseph Killorin, Armstrong State College; Maurine
H. Klein, College of St. Elizabeth; Edwin B. Knowles, Pratt Institute;
Stanley Koehler, University of Massachusetts; Leonard Michael Koff,
Columbia University; Maurice Kramer, Brooklyn College; Lincoln F.
Ladd, University of North Carolina, Greensboro; Parker B. Ladd,
Charles Scribner's Sons; Rev. John P. Lahey, s.j., Le Moyne College;
Lewis Leary, Columbia University; Francis Noel Lees, University of
Manchester; Simon D. Lesser, University of Massachusetts; David
Levin, Stanford University; Lois Lewin, Carnegie Institute of Tech-
nology; Piers I. Lewis, Wellesley College; Dwight N. Lindley,
Hamilton College; Mark Linenthal, San Francisco State College;
Carol A. Locke, New York City; George de F. Lord, Yale Univer-
sity; J. P. Lovering, Canisius College; Fei-Pai Lu, C. W. Post Col-
lege; Sister Mary Aloyse Lubin, College of St. Elizabeth; Isabel G.
MacCaffrey, Bryn Mawr College; Julia H. McGrew, Vassar College;
Mary A. McGuire, Chatham College; Louise B. Mackenzie, Wheaton
College; Richard A. Macksey, The Johns Hopkins University; Ken-
neth MacLean, University of Toronto; Lorna E. MacLean, Sir
George Williams University; William G. Madsen, Emory Univer-
sity; Mother C. E. Maguire, Newton College of the Sacred Heart;
Harold C. Martin, Union College; Jay Martin, Yale University;
Dorothy Mateer, College of Wooster; Robert D. Mayo, Northwest-
ern University; John A. Meixner, University of Kansas; Donald C.
Mell, Jr., Middlebury College; John H. Middendorf, Columbia Uni-
versity; Gretchen Mieszkowski, New Haven, Connecticut; J. Hillis
Miller, The Johns Hopkins University; Sister Jeanne Pierre Mitt-
night, c.s.j., The College of St. Rose; Mother Grace Monahan, o.s.u.,
College of New Rochelle; Robert L. Montgomery, University of
Texas; William T. Moynihan, University of Connecticut; William
Nelson, Columbia University; Helaine Newstead, Hunter College;
Rev. William T. Noon, s.j., Le Moyne College; Sister M. Norma,

Albertus Magnus College; William B. Ober, M.D., New York Medical College; Paul E. O'Connell, Prentice-Hall, Inc.; Gerald O'Grady, Rice University; Mme J. Ollier, Université de Nice; Rev. Joseph E. O'Neill, s.j., Fordham University; Ants Oras, University of Florida; Mother Thomas Aquinas O'Reilly, o.s.u., College of New Rochelle; James M. Osborn, Yale University; Charles A. Owen, Jr., University of Connecticut; Stephen C. Paine, Bradley University; Rev. Adrian J. Parcher, o.s.b., St. Martin's College; Coleman O. Parsons, City College of New York; Richard Pearce, Wheaton College; Roy Harvey Pearce, University of California, San Diego; Norman Holmes Pearson, Yale University; Harry William Pedicord, Thiel College; Margaret W. Pepperdene, Agnes Scott College; Gerald H. Perkus, Babson Institute; Henry H. Peyton III, Southeastern Massachusetts Technical Institute; Sister St. Pierre, College of New Rochelle; Raymond J. Porter, Iona College; Annis Pratt, Emory University; K. R. Pringle, Kent State University; Richard E. Quaintance, Jr., Douglass College; Esther C. Quinn, Hunter College; Virginia L. Radley, Russell Sage College; Paul Ramsey, University of Chattanooga; Ralph A. Ranald, New York University; Isabel E. Rathborne, Hunter College; Donald H. Reiman, The Carl H. Pforzheimer Library; Edmund Reiss, Pennsylvania State University; Sister Richard Mary, o.p., Albertus Magnus College; Sister Rita Margaret, o.p., Caldwell College for Women; William R. Robinson, University of Virginia; Leo Rockas, New York State University College, Geneseo; Sister Rose Bernard Donna, c.s.j., The College of St. Rose; Claire Rosenfield, Rutgers University; Mel Rosenthal, University of Connecticut; Rebecca D. Ruggles, Brooklyn College; Muriel Rukeyser, Sarah Lawrence College; Iva Jones Sawyer, Morgan State College; Bernard N. Schilling, University of Rochester; Helene B. M. Schnabel, New York City; Robert Scholes, University of Iowa; H. T. Schultz, Dartmouth College; Susan Field Senneff, Bronxville, New York; Frank E. Seward, The Catholic University of America; Richard Sexton, Fordham University; Stephen Shapiro, University of California, Irvine; John T. Shawcross, Douglass College; Gordon M. Shedd, Pennsylvania State University; John D. Simmonds, University of

Pittsburgh; Joseph Evans Slate, University of Texas; Nelle Smither, Douglass College; George Soule, Carleton College; Ian Sowton, University of Alberta; J. Gordon Spaulding, University of British Columbia; Ann Stanford, San Fernando Valley State College; S. Susan Stave, University of Virginia; Oliver Steele, University of Virginia; Maureen T. Sullivan, University of Pennsylvania; William P. Sullivan, The College of St. Rose; Joseph H. Summers, Washington University; Donald R. Swanson, Upsala College; J. C. Thirlwall, City College of New York; Jonathan Thomas, Trenton State College; Wright Thomas, New York State University College, Cortland; Doris Stevens Thompson, Russell Sage College; Lawrance Thompson, Princeton University; Richard J. Thompson, Canisius College; R. C. Townsend, Amherst College; Donald Tritschler, Skidmore College; Mary Curtis Tucker, Marietta, Georgia; Dale Underwood, University of New Hampshire; A. D. Van Nostrand, Brown University; David M. Vieth, Southern Illinois University; Howard P. Vincent, Kent State University; Sister M. Vivien, o.p., Caldwell College for Women; Eugene M. Waith, Yale University; Andrew J. Walker, Georgia Institute of Technology; Mother B. Walsh, Academy of the Sacred Heart; Herbert Weil, Jr., University of Connecticut; Jeanne K. Welcher, Forest Hills, New York; James J. Wey, University of Detroit; Reed Whittemore, Carleton College; Brother Joseph Wiesenfarth, f.s.c., Manhattan College; Elizabeth Wiley, Susquehanna University; Margaret Lee Wiley, University of Texas, Arlington; Roger B. Wilkenfeld, University of Connecticut; Mary Denise Wilkens, Southampton College; Maurita Willett, University of Illinois; Lyle Givens Williams, University of Southwestern Louisiana; Marilyn L. Williamson, Oakland University; W. K. Wimsatt, Yale University; Calhoun Winton, University of Delaware; Ross Woodman, University of Western Ontario; Carl Woodring, Columbia University; Daniel H. Woodward, Mary Washington College; Samuel K. Workman, Newark College of Engineering; William H. Youngren, Massachusetts Institute of Technology; Larzer Ziff, University of California, Berkeley; Rose Zimbardo, City College of New York.